the life of the theatre

BAte, Dops - 1·8·71

julian beck

the life of the theatre
the relation of
the artist to the struggle
of the people

new foreword by Judith Malina

LIMELIGHT EDITIONS

First Limelight Edition May 1986

Parts of this book first appeared in *Kulchur, Yale Drama Review, Teatro, Fuck You/A Magazine of the Arts,* and *Bastard Angel.*

Cover photo by Alair Gomes, Rio de Janeiro
Sketch of Julian Beck (frontispiece) by Guido Rocha

Library of Congress Cataloging-in-Publication Data

Beck, Julian.
    The life of the theatre.
    Reprint. Originally published: San Francisco,
Calif.: City Lights, ©1972.
    1. Theater—Literary collections.   2. Living
Theatre (New York, N.Y.)   I. Title.
PS3552.E247L5   1986   818'.5403   86-2939
ISBN 0-87910-062-1

CONTENTS: THE PLOT

Foreword to the New Edition of The Life of the Theatre

"Death is corruption and is not intrinsic to life." I cannot contend against this contradiction. Julian Beck, whose banner was the conquest of death by the awakening of the people's revolutionary spirit through the struggle of the artist, loved to quote this uncompromising declaration by the prophet-philosopher Eric Gutkind.

At this writing the philosopher Gutkind is dead many years and Julian Beck only a few months.

What speaks for them—after the victory of corruption, that is, death—are the immortal words, and would Eurydice have harrowed hell had Orpheus died? But no, he could not die, because the uncorrupted message makes its way to us, full of enigmas (for therein lies the poetry), through endless vistas charged with locks and doors and keys.

"The manufacture of keys is the work of the artist," said Julian. . . . "Open the doors."

Therefore we may draw the conclusion that we must, even that we *can*, contend against this contradiction: that we choose life, but are swallowed up, unwillingly, by death. . . .

"The contradiction of my life: the contradiction of this book: this book is the plea of my life to myself . . ." But the key is the structure: "Commentary: This book (this writing of mine, *The Life of the Theatre*) is it a seduction . . .? Do we cut ourselves off from the people when we speak to each other in such coded symbols?" But it is precisely the decoding of these "symbols" that constitutes the process of revolutionary awakening.

The search for the key to decoding is written into the structure of the book. He begins, "We live in a system that manufactures sorrow . . . and we drown down, dead, too soon." So on the brink of submersion he sets out for "the reversal of the system" and the "turning of the tides."

He begins with being a slave in Egypt, as our Haggadah does—its story, too, the recital of a prison break, at a meal called the seder, meaning order, or sequence: another code for the liberation strategy, contained in a mystery—and he concludes with "break out of the prison, the theatre, into the world."

The image is the image of the jailbreak: the reasons for its urgency; the forms it could take; the inspirations from which it draws its strength; the planning; the most precise and explicitly wrought preparations; the hopes for its accomplishment; the visions of a future without prison's constraints; warnings; hints; messages, historical and futuristic; the anticipation of the joys of liberty.

"Do I have a map? No. 1969. Wait a few years." "How do we rob death of its power?" "Always the same beautiful question."

Julian affirmed that the highest art shall be best understood by the most oppressed, because of their need. And with all the means of art, as writer, poet, activist, man of the theatre, street performer, painter, actor, anarchist spokesman, playwright, rebel lover and pacifist agitator, with all the means of art he roused us from the torpor of our fear. He made the theatre the matrix, the model, the prophetic vision of revolutionary action that could be liberatory without being destructive.

He stood in the doorway, tore through the curtains, "cut the curtains" and beckoned us. Beckoned us to enter "where no one can go thru alone."

"The artist," he whispered to me in the dead of the Morroccan night, where we were forbidden on pain of expulsion or prison to show our plays, even gratis on the roof of our house to the sons of slaves. . . .

"The artist," he gasped in the sunlit bullring, where compassion seemed in combat with glory . . .

"The artist," he said defiantly, in the cell of the torture house in the prison in Brazil in the dread days of the military dictatorship, where the walls were spattered with the blood of the last victim, "The artist is a maker of maps. We will draw up the map for the liberation of dreams: the transformation of ideas into working acts."

"how do we open the doors of all the jails?" "the purpose of the theatre is to open the doors of all the jails."

The description of the prison break: "barbed wire . . . walls . . . barriers . . . prison world . . . locked in . . . locked in . . . doors . . . trapped . . . locked in . . . locked in . . . locked in . . . open the doors of the world prison. . . . This book is a movie ten years in the making. . . . The process of breaking through the barriers . . . and beyond the code in which it is written." Then follow the strategies. When the Brazilian police allowed us to meet in the torture cells of the Department of Political and Social Order, in Belo Horizonte, where some dozen sections of *The Life of the Theatre* were written on the louse-infected mats, Julian said: "Here we will plot the peaceable revolution. It is called the M.A.P., the acronym, the secret acronym of the Movimento Anarco-Pacifista."

That was in 1971 . . . And now in 1986 we have arrived at a moment in history when we witness the apparent triumph of materialism over that "utopian dream" . . . that . . . "draws us always on." And we need to reexamine and redefine these words once again: "movement" and "anarchist" and "pacifist."

"This book," Julian wrote as we traveled between Aix-en-Provence and Avignon with our busload of actors and children, "this examination: it is to find out if it is true that everything conceived in terms of theatre . . . can be tuned . . . until it declares its affinity with the revolutionary proposals of anarchism and violentless human relations."

The Life of the Theatre was written twice. The first version fell into the hands of a thief in the city of Fontainebleau, snatched away in a little garden in front of our hotel; in the flick of an eye, gone, the work of five years. "What a fortuitous occurrence," said the optimistic Julian, "for now I will write it as it should be . . . I know so much more." And he began to make notes anew: "Pause and begin again . . ." His life so full and rich that there was only the stolen moment for the notebooks, written while running, but meditated upon on the long roads up and down Europe, or in the cells, or the dressing rooms . . .

"We who want to burn the texts and read them too. The Tree of Knowledge and the Tree of Life."

What is left now of Julian's bold rejection of death? Can I believe that his great hope is unfulfilled? No, not I. "The hope that we shall one day see together the beautiful nonviolent anarchist revolution." But note the structure: This dedication, which customarily comes at the very beginning, he has placed to follow the section that starts, "I tremble that all this might someday shatter and fade away . . ." And it is followed, by the most fundamental of directions, brief as signposts in the wilderness, the way to go, and that ends with the injunction to "do it."

What is left now for Julian's sumptuous poetry is that we make of it a map, that we make use of it to "break out of the prison, the theatre, into the world."

If you can find the path through this structure, and see that it is not a labyrinth, but by your moving through it, construct the rationale of the concrete suggestions so that they are not in conflict with, but rather that they speak for, the poetry; if you can feel the unity of what has been dispersed, combative, competitive, and gather the forces, we will yet fulfill this prophecy. Here is the M.A.P.

Judith Malina

January 1, 1986
New York City

the life of the theatre

1

There is a misery of the body and a misery of the mind, and if the stars, whenever we looked at them, poured nectar into our mouths, and the grass became bread, men would still be sad. We live in a system that manufactures sorrow, spilling it out of its mill, the waters of sorrow, ocean, storm, and we drown down, dead, too soon.

Theatre is like a boat, it is only so big, but uprising is the reversal of the system, and revolution is the turning of tides.

Ouro Preto, Brazil. 6 May 1971

2

I am a slave who came out of Egypt. I have a slave mentality. Out of the house of bondage, into the house of employment. What an illusion, three thousand five hundred years ago, when we moved out of one culture into another, thinking we were going to be our own masters from then on! We got rid of a political master, and were too inexperienced to recognize the true function of the Paymaster, the Chief of Police, the Pillars of Society.

The prediction (when we were dancing around the Golden Calf): precious stones, warships, waste, doom, etc. We have not yet stopped dancing around that false god, metal, that does not feel, Mammon, idol of riches, and that's why we are still in the desert. When we entered the Promised Land we carried the Golden Calf with us, not on our backs, but in our hearts, and made the Promised Land into the desert, which is the only place where the Golden Calf ever is: because the radiance of the gold (radiation) dessicates the foliage, dries up the rivers (the blood), and the vessicles of the heart. The Golden Calf is the false promise.

Among my brethren are many who dream with wet pleasure of the eight hundred pains and humiliations, but I am the other kind: I am a slave who dreams of escape after escape, I dream only of escaping, ascent, of a thousand possible ways to make a hole in the wall, of melting the bars, escape escape, of burning the whole prison down if necessary.

Croissy-sur-Seine, France. April 1970.

3

Frankenstein. Act III.

Violent revolution breaks out in the world prison. It is Victor Frankenstein's final solution, his last desperate attempt to resolve the question, "How can we end human suffering?" And the whole world burns down; and out of the ashes the Creature forms itself again and menaces, with searchlight and net, the whole world. Suddenly: mutation: the Creature drops the net and the searchlight, raises both arms to the sky, the head tilts upwards, Humankind Lives, it is hope. Because we believe that the miraculous will somehow occur. Because if we do burn down the world in revolution, with violence, then only a miracle, mutation, will provide life.

The Creature, at the end of the first act and of the third act, is formed of dead bodies which are the victims of the social structure. The Creature that comes into being formed out of the charred bodies at the end of the third act is indeed ourselves, but as we will be, at the end of a violent revolution, charred, scarred, disfigured, ready to threaten and menace, to be salvaged only by mutation.

This image of hope in the midst of so much despair is mandatory in the revolution's catechism. Because despair annihilates all action.

Brooklyn, New York City. October 1968.

2

4

The Creature who is formed at the end of the first and third acts of *Frankenstein* not only menaces the public, it is the public. The Creature simultaneously menaces civilization and is civilization, it is civilization menacing itself.

That is, we are both civilization and the monster that threatens civilization, and within us is the creature who raises his arms and breathes, conspicuously changing and transforming, and praying for the next development in humanity.

Lausanne, Switzerland. 10 January 1968.

5

1: The imagination as the survival kit of the brain.

2: The work of the artist as the creation of solutions thru the exercise of the imagination.

We are waiting for certain answers. But the new artists say that there can be no leaders. End of Moses. Disappearance of Lao-tzu into the people.

The oil of my imagination is my slave mentality.

This is a book about the role of the artist in the revolution.

Croissy-sur-Seine, France. April 1970.

6

Meditation. 1961. New York City.

I am a man not interested in theatre. The entertainments that demean our being. The dissemination of lies. Fun is destructive while joy creates. Eric Gutkind.

Life is being dreamed. An old mirage while we live in the desert. My whole life is a dream. Strindberg. We are dreaming one another. We go in and out of existence each moment. Have will and am willed. Each day I know less and less. This is my glory.

The theatre of our time pretends to know too much. Most of what we think we comprehend is false. We don't have enough facts, the vision is too limited, we are not free to see. Nor think. When the actor is free, like any man, he can create, yet we go to the theatre and bear to watch actors fettered by the madness of the bourgeoisie whose madness is its laws which are its life, a life of money which is also a law and drives men mad. Freedom now in its infancy and may die still a babe, and civilization, like the universe, rapidly expanding, and civilization but a child, and may die still a child. 1961 is not the pinnacle. Nor even dates we can't imagine. We go on forever tho death exists. Suicide exists too; choose life. If I want to preserve the world it's my own life I immortalize. As long as men live so do we all.

Narrow vision. Men vary. Huts and turrets. Rice and telephones. And no man differs more from another than from himself at some other time. Pascal.

The theatre is a dream. It, like a dream, an image of the world. The world interests me. "M. Dali," said his companion, "is interested in everything." "Why is your work so concerned with poverty?" and, leaning over the table, Dali asked Allen Ginsberg, "Is not gold the measure of genius?" Genius yes, concentrated creators among us, they keep the world in constant creation, but the people keep the world fed.

My conscience reels under the impact of the Jewish sky and that banner of the rabbonim on which it is proclaimed that the world is in the process of creation and that it is man's sacred duty to assist God in this process.

Buber speaks of "nearness to God" as "the difference between true existence and mere conscious being."

To all sides of a thing at one time. Levels. Simultaneity.

The great preoccupying discovery of the twentieth century. Unification impossible without it. Divided men never find the golden answer. My unique life.

One life. Woe is me. Choice. Shall I go to the Gaspé. Shall I be a salesman or a buyer. Shall I till the earth, feed the poor, add the accounts for merchants and friends, shall I tear up the world and make dust of the plumage, turn the rocks and rills to decomposing blood, infanticide, germicide, shall I pasteurize milk, or paint farting dolls, sleep with men, sleep with women, disturb, tranquilize, bestialize, love, sacrifice, write, torment, augment, embrace, water, or decay. Shall I grow old or grow wise.

I do not choose to work in the theatre but in the world. The Living Theatre has become my life the living theatre. We devour each other. I can't tell one from the other. Judith and I merge in it. Others with us. There are actors who hang on like Jeffers' lice on the eagle. There are actors who are my eyes and technicians who are our wings. The nest we build may crawl with maggots. The eggs breed carnivores. My theatre. I hold up the mirror till my arms ache. It falls on the heads of the spectators, leaving them bleeding and marred. Or it does nothing. I hold up a mirror which is only a crumbling ikon of shit, and I am buried under it. A mound of dung upon the stage where no man ought to look. A unique life of nothing.

How can I tell. All I can do is worry, never tell.

On the stage there is life. An actor who brings back from his adventures a moment of communicable penetration is a hero, the light of our lives.

I go to the theatre instead of to the synagogue. Not to worship but to discover the way to salvation. I might find the experience of my life. I will soar, actually levitate like Horatio in Paul Goodman's *The Dead of Spring*. He taught me.

Worship doesn't look like salvation.

By observing what is beautiful we can learn what is meant to be. Judith.

Derived from the spell of God, spelled with God, aimed at God, fulfilled by men set out for glory. The ancients played in sunlight, we in electric light, light is the clothing of glory, though darkness has its day.

Passion. Agony, Despair. Work. The work, the hammers, the persistence, the brooms, the nails unite me with men, else I'd be but poetry and flight. I'd be no good alone. The theatre is an exercise in pure community. No one man can do it, made by many, for many. But life on the kibbutz is tough. Everyone complains. I most of all. There is no help for it, but it is as perfect as the weather, always beautiful, like a calendar, always terrible, the day always dies, the sun disappears, the wind is wild and west.

I work out my life in the theatre. With Judith, the angel of my life, without whom there would be no Living Theatre ever.

Je ne trouve pas, je cherche.

7

Meditation. 1962. New York City.

Someday we will have to account for our premature death. Artaud.

You must enter the theatre through the world.

It is the holy mission that redeems the theatre.

Everything exists, nothing has value. Without value there are errors, sins, losses.

In the secret quarters, in the underground, in Greenwich Village, Saint Germain, among the campus students planning sit-ins and freedom rides, in the hidden quarters of Africa, wherever change is initiated, in the music of changes, in the march to the sea, in the picket lines in front of embassies, the worth of the world is proclaimed. In the invisible lofts where the anarchists and pacifists defy money and the structure of society, where the lies are being examined and reversed, lies which are the allies of death, in these places is the poetry which is the language of God.

In madness which is the force that delivers us to the rim of the sphere in which we're encased, the sphere in which we die, the sphere that floats in the unreckoned universe which we are denied until we let the vision of the madness-force, Ginsberg, assist us to pass thru the wall of the sphere, puncture, into the creation of which we have only heard archetypal rumors. When the madness-force has done its work and we have learned to breathe.

Our way of life is not to be defended, the way of premature death, death from government, death from weapons, death from oppression, death from class, death from the draft, death from poverty, death from racist stomp, death from law, death from police, death from fallout, poison in the air, death from education, the terrible icebox death, death from wellbeing, death from possessions, death from falsehood, the pain in my stomach, the cancer in my back, the plagues that wrack the bodies more and more ill-made for living, the loss of being.

The falsehood of ideals. Death from Broadway. Ideal clothing, ideal speech. Death from compromise, certain death from luxury and lack of it. Aspects of the stage that are not the world but vanity. This is the vanity stage against which we have pitted our being, not yet knowing what tools to use, nor how to use them, unsafe, witless, a barefoot army of stragglers.

I do not like the Broadway theatre because it does not know how to say hello. The tone of voice is false, the mannerisms are false, the sex is false, ideal, the Hollywood world of perfection, the clean image, the well pressed clothes, the well scrubbed anus, odorless, inhuman, of the Hollywood actor, the Broadway star. And the terrible false dirt of Broadway, the lower depths in which the dirt is imitated, inaccurate.

The acting at The Living Theatre has been despised for many years, particularly by other actors. Judith and I have worked to build a company without the mannerisms, the voices, the good speech, the protective coloring of the actors who imitate the world of the White House and who enact the trifles and suffering of the bourgeoisie. The world of conscious experience is not enough.

The actors at The Living Theatre are awkward, untutored, unconsciously defiant of the conventions which portray the people who live in democracies, who are rational, good, well balanced, and who speak museum verse. The actors at The Living Theatre want to be concerned with life and death.

The acting at The Living Theatre is only a hesitant gesture, an implication of further development, as if arms might become wings, legs fins, bodies something undreamed of. Something else. The Broadway theatre seeks what it would like to see. What is surpasses all illusion. "Accuracies." William Carlos Williams.

You enter the theatre through the world, world that is holy, world that is imperfect, you enter the theatre through awareness of the indestructible ugliness. Life ugliness. You embrace that ugliness and forget what is beautiful. The way of transcendence. The Acropolis, all that striving, all that striving for the perfection myth, will dissolve in the mass of being which is goodness.

Can't care about anything else.

Ameliorative theatre. In which it is possible to discover someone sitting on the toilet without embarrassment.

Rejection of all those who proclaim thru the convention of their playwriting the conventions of civilization, the ways to premature death. All or nothing.

The Living Theatre is at best an imitation, feeble, longing, corrupt, power-principled, dictatorial, arrogant, uncommunal, it yearns for the day when it will wither away. In this is its only opposition to Broadway, demon of the upper world, demon of the money changers, who seek to improve the value of the dollar, who accept a world of premature death. They are Errico Malatesta's "man in chains" (people so accustomed to walking in bonds that they cannot believe it would be easier without them).

All niceness must then be exploded.

Le Rappel à l'ordre. All the pseudo organization must be scattered. And when the wind of Greenwich Village has done its work, after the breaking up of illusion, the broken pieces may penetrate, puncture the outer universe where death is no longer the answer and the conclusion.

Every time the curtain rises on a Broadway play I strike my forehead with the palm of my hand, $100,000 for what? Harold Rosenberg.

A setting that is "order," whose "order" denies the order of things as they are, whose most advanced design at best reflects a piquant balance, sentimental color. Sentiment, which is the substitution of false feeling for real (when nothing else can be felt).

Excellent form is a lie.

Too much perfection on Broadway. They make a graven image, all, all of them vanity; and their delectable things shall not profit; and they are their own witness; they see not, nor know; that they may be ashamed. The smith that maketh an axe and worketh it in the coals, and worketh it with the strength of his arms, yea he is hungry and his strength faileth. He that heweth down cedars; yea he maketh a god and worshippeth it, he maketh a graven image, and boweth down thereto. They have not known nor understood, they cannot see. He feedeth on ashes, a deceived heart hath turned his aside that he cannot deliver his soul, nor say, Is there not a lie in my right hand? Isaiah.

"Ameliorative theatre. To make something useful." Judith.

To make something useful. Nothing else is interesting. Nothing else is interesting to the audience, the great audience. To serve the audience, to instruct, to excite sensation, to initiate experience, to awaken awareness, to make the heart pound, the blood course, the tears flow, the voice shout, to circle round the altar, the muscles move in laughter, the body feel, to be released from death's ways, deterioration in comfort. To provide the useful event that can help us. Help.

I indulge in this polemic because it is the only thing worth saying. The journey to love is not romantic. Out of my negation will come the way to endless positive creation. Help.

8

Meditation I. 1963. New York City.

Dreams of a free society.

Within that free society the dream of a theatre which is useful. The dream of useful things in an epoch congested with useless things. Given enough time everything is interesting. As long as it's interesting. John Cage. But there isn't enough time.

Useless production, useless laws, useless forms. The world wide money prison, wages prison, a life of buying things not needed, making things not needed, getting and spending laying waste our powers. Interesting, but not enough. My chant.

Useless theatre. Begin with examination of the architecture. Is this a place for human beings, this insinuation of plush and gold, this staircase pomp, this chandelier delusion grandeur, this modern theatre art design? O architecture of potentates! O reek of money! Is this where the Bird in Space has flown? Where are the dockers, the textile workers, the mechanics? There are no farmers here, no one who built this building, none who grow the food, there are no blacks here, no one who cleans a sewer, no one who sews the seams. Whom is this building for? Where are the people? What is happening here that it does not speak to them? The carpet is made for pale patrician feet, the seats provide a comfort alien to action, retarding participation, indulging the passive body. Walls of seclusion! O may our loud harangue cause the walls to tremble and fall, fall prisons, fall fortresses of false industry, fall all houses of separation. Unity. That is, when the people are together and not set against one another there is that harmony which dispels despair, extends being, and makes possible all the impossible hopes.

When I sit down in the velour seat surrounded by celanese acetate, if a person cries out, if a man dies, it only interrupts. I am not prepared to react to life. I only watch. Surrounded by cold companions in an atmosphere of deceit, I sit in pomp. Have I come here to die, frozen? How can I break thru to feeling? I am invested rayonese royalty, how can I transcend in velvet surroundings, how can I find the key in this dark room? Only if I dream. But this dream is a lie, I feel nothing. It is all

10

lies, it is fleshless, and fundamentally sexless. And by being there I make it happen.

States dictate to the artist and everyone else. Good bad should shouldn't. Of this, democracy feigns disdain; nevertheless the capitalist theatre is not uncontrolled. The rod of money, the rule of the investor, the vote of the conforming spectator. If we want a free theatre we must make it free. First of all we have to make it free to the audience, no money to get in, without Mammon's measure, life at last.

The theatre of exclusion where no black people come, where we have white closed thoughts and frozen feeling. I know that I am not superior, but we make an experience that excludes the poor, satisfying ourselves that the poor don't want it. When I go to the theatre I am cut off from the poor. There is something wrong when I go to the theatre whose province is the world and instead of being brought closer to the world I am cut off from it.

We are a feelingless people. If we could really feel, the pain would be so great that we would stop all the suffering. If we could feel that one person every six seconds dies of starvation, (and as this is happening, this writing, this reading, someone is dying of starvation) we would stop it. If we could really feel it in the bowels, the groin, in the throat, in the breast, we would go into the streets and stop the war, stop slavery, stop the prisons, stop the killings, stop destruction. Ah, I might learn what love is.

Joy. St. Theresa's cherished virtue. Joy. In the theatre we might feel it in communion with each other. I would make plays not of sorrows, of problems, nor tough opinions, but of joy, pleasure, laughter, exultation, not cruel laughter, not satire, but joy. But hard to feel joy, hard therefore ever to know joy, when you are pale and the world is outside and dying. Wanting a different theatre worthy of what we really are, expecting that the theatre will change, but what we really want is that we change, that in conjunction with one another we all change, and in changing, change the world.

11

9

Meditation II. 1963. New York City

what is happening is happening in our theatre because
it accepts the patterns of procedure of a homicidal society
and makes them seem admirable
it also make much of trivia
in a life of tribulation
makes the intolerable seem tolerable
makes life seem entertaining and amusing and gives easy answers
and when i ask why do the spectators permit this to happen
i sadly see that it is indeed
because this life we are leading is becoming unbearable
and the deceit on the stages
is a comfort
tho no one believes it
but people prefer to pretend that it's true because then things
     are maybe not so bad
and thus the theatre of our time is a place of fraudulence
     and misrepresentation
what is happening there is deception for the middle class and
     aristocracy who want to be deceived
if you want to see the truth you have to be mad mad enough to
     confront a horror

Experiences, autobiography: If you want to know me come and live with me.

First plans for a theatre—twenty, twenty-one years old. Disinterested in the theatre of that time, portraiture of sub-human people, and patriotic too, patriotism as a fool's pastime except for that passion for the land and its people which is a lover's passion. Why the mere image of the theatre of our time is enough to precipitate a revolution.

In anger we began. All the sane theatre of that time was beneath the dignity of childbearing women and vigorous men. Anything happening worthy of the spectator was a kind of insane thing, gestures scooped from the actor's entrails, unconscious like the reflex motions of grasshoppers, the appendages twitching as pins slip thru the thorax, hands of the drowning, things like anonymous messages received during sleep.

We watched for things driven thru the fuse of the imagination gone wild, escaping. Those were the things the only things that beaconed from the abode where the immortals are.

Take the cue. Go into the madhouse and find out the truth: in the imbalance of the order of things, in the perversity of real love, in the bursting cysts of the mind. No more deception. If you want to see what's what, you have to be mad, able to confront the horror.

We went to the theatre all the time, Judith and I. Everything was interesting and infuriating. Two three four times a week. So that by 1946 Judith knew that she didn't want to work in that theatre. I, hung up on painting at that time, took six months to come in on it, and we said we'd make a theatre that would do something else. Now, fifteen years later, we know we haven't. We also believed that there was some kind of sociological lag in the development of the theatre. That is, we were reading Joyce and Pound, Breton, Lorca, Proust, Patchen, Goodman, Cummings, Stein, Rilke, Cocteau, und so weiter. 1944: the painting of Pollock and De Kooning was implying a life which the theatre didn't know existed, a level of consciousness and unconsciousness that rarely found itself onto the stage. Judith studied with Piscator who knew that radical politics and social action were the Way. We talked about Anarchism, Marxism, Greek myths and metres, dreams and Freud, youthful talks, and walked in the woods along the Palisades, and went to the sea a lot, beach beauty. Perhaps our most profound understanding: that the 1940's were not the pinnacle of human achievement, and yet that in the 1940's was, dispersed, all the glory the world would ever contain. The problem of finding, assorting, reassembling matter, feeling, and being. A theatre for that.

You are what you eat and what you won't eat anymore.

I ate an entire handkerchief bit by bit at the age of six at a Metropolitan Opera performance of Hansel and Gretel. It is an opera much concerned with eating, candy houses, hungry children, breadcrumbs, fattening of Hansel and Gretel, cannibal witch who eats children. My father thought I was eating because I was nervous, which was true, but I was also eating along with Hansel to identify with him, the tasteless awful handkerchief—and then I didn't have to eat it anymore, all the children were free, out of the oven, uneaten, alive, and still to grow up. Everything I have ever done in the theatre has been an attempt to free the yearning for freedom from the witch's prison cage, which the Hansel and Gretel experience gave me. The event convinced me of three needs in the theatre for total experience: physical participation by the spectator participant, narrative, and transcendence-which-is-revolution.

Narrative is important in the theatre because if the theatre is to be the world it cannot neglect what happens, the passing from one moment to the next. Specialized experience like sponges of blue ink tossed onto green glass can fascinate eyes, but the person who throws the sponge is always more interesting than the splashing ink. The problem is to make a theatre in which this is clear. Your hand lifting the familiar coffee cup to your lips is more than a vermillion streak in the evening sky: whatever you do beats any scenery, this must be made clear. If we are to survive the landscape.

When we went to Robert Edmond Jones in 1947 to tell him about our theatre he got very excited and asked us to come back again.

We did, I brought him my stage designs and we talked about plays we were planning to do. We talked a lot, he looked very sad and we asked him why. At first, he said, I thought you had the answer, that you were really about to create the new theatre, but I see that you are only asking the questions. How much money do you have? $6,000, I said. That's too bad, he said, I wish you had no money, no money at all, perhaps then you would create the new theatre, make your theatre out of string and sofa cushions, make it in studios and living rooms. Forget the big theatres, he said, and the paid admissions, nothing is happening there, nothing can happen there that is not stultifying, nothing will ever come out of it. Here, if you want, take this room, he said, offering us his studio, if you want to begin here you can have it.

It was not until four years later, unable to locate a theatre in which to work that we decided to do some plays in our own living room and not charge a cent nor spend a cent. It worked, he was right. But we still had not thoroly understood. Therefore we have had theatres which advertise commercially and charge admission and pay taxes, as if those things made something happen, la gloire perhaps. Into the trap. Recognizing that we are in it we are at last beginning to discuss strategies for getting out.

there is something awry when the paintings of picasso and the
        music of schoenberg
are emblazoned on the coats of arms of the power elite
rockefeller collects de kooning
on wall street they read allen ginsberg

jacqueline kennedy adores manet
they are taking everything away

Malraux and Frost sold their birthrights by serving the state with the excuse of trying to popularize national art. The state does not wish to bring art to the people, it seeks diamonds in its crown. Now what is really happening when the Elysée Palace names a lobster after Claudel is that art is being stolen, de-balled, and served up as chocolate. Spain now lures tourists with pictures of its great artists, Picasso, but not *Guernica*, not the *Dreams and Lies of Franco;* Lorca, but not the body of his work nor his body. Cocteau has said that the revolutionary artist is first ignored, then scorned, and when these things do not work they try to suppress you by loading you down with honors.

theoretically you should not be able to like de kooning and build
        bomb shelters (as rockefeller does)
you cannot approve yevtushenko and stockpile bombs (as khruschev
        does)
art must either oppose the state or destroy its own life force
when the state heaps honors on art it is a way of saying this
        art is safe for the ruling class
beware of approval and official support

dorothy day at the *catholic worker* has spent thirty years living
        in voluntary poverty and feeding and clothing and housing
        the poor
and when the fund for the republic a division of the ford foundation
        offered her $10,000 i believe i may be wrong the sum may even
        have been larger but not smaller
the *catholic worker* refused it
because they would not take blood money
that is they would not take money that had been extorted from people
        thru the devices of interest and investment and war production
        and the cruelty of factory labor
and use that money to feed the poor because by accepting that money
        they would be assuaging the guilt of the system that is killing
        us off and is producing the misery the catholic workers
        are trying to ease
in our hard society in these hard times it is hard for people to
        understand this

i have even known people to express rage as if dorothy day (and not
            the vicious nature of money) had robbed the poor of bread because
            the *catholic worker* refused to accept blood money
this is because people are always thinking about the expedient
and do not know that you really cannot accomplish good thru bad
that is also why people think that a theatre which gives them
            something to think about, the intellectual theatre popular today,
is a good thing
but a theatre which accepts support from a society which is adamantly
            opposed to
change
is the theatre of the finks
it is a mechanism for making a bad thing shrewder and stronger
the patient is dying and we are putting bandaids on the wounds
the people will tolerate much until they can tolerate too much
            no longer
in the theatre we are beginning to approach that stage
the stage on which too much is no longer tolerable
and something else must happen

10

questions. 1963.

i end with questions because i have no answers.

of three broadcasts on the life of the theatre delivered over station wbai
new york city this was the third.

what is the difference between questions and answers

is hamlet questioning his glory or his tragedy

why do you go to the theatre

is it important to go to the theatre

is it important to read

do people who go to the theatre differ from people who don't go to
        the theatre

what happens to you if you go to the theatre

when you leave the theatre have you changed that is of course you are
        changed by each moment of experience so three hours later you
        are naturally different but i mean have you changed actively

do you want to change actively

are you content

is it good to change

is anything sufficient unchanged

what am i talking about

do you go to the theatre for answers

do you have any questions

how long is a lifetime

does it matter what happens

does it matter how long we live

does it matter how we live

why do i ask these simple questions that everyone must be asking all
the time is it because i think you don't ask these questions

what is happening to us

what happens in the theatre

do you go to the theatre to find out about life

is it easier to observe life in the theatre or in the street

have you experienced joy in the threatre

have you experienced joy in the street

what do you enjoy

do you get sensual sensations in the theatre

do you go to the theatre for sexual stimulation

do you like rubbing up against the person next to you

do you go to the theatre for intellectual exercises

do you go to the theatre to find out if it has figured out what
     is going on

do you go to the theatre because it might be telling the truth

is anything that is the truth

are newspapers the truth

do playwrights record the truth more than editors

do newspapers lie do playwrights lie do actors lie

do playwrights or editors or actors lie deliberately

do you go to the theatre to see how well an actor can disguise
     himself as somebody else

do you think that actors should try to personify excellent being

what is excellent being

can an actor show you excellent being

can an actor show excellent being only when playing faust

what is insight

do you use your insight

is it easy to ask questions

what did aristotle say about catharsis

do you go to the theatre for a purge

do you ever remember being purged in the theatre

do you go to the theatre with expectancy and hope

is the theatre a way of learning things you do not know

what is learning for

are you certain of any answers

are all things equal

does anything have value

is it all right to kill sometimes

what is the difference between an elephant and a handkerchief

should you kill someone to defend your property

should you put people in jail

do you make fun of homosexuals

do you think black people are just a little inferior

do you think white people are decaying physically and mentally

do you lie

does it matter if you lie

how many times a day do you lie

do you find that you have to lie to get along in this world

are you content i ask again

are you content with anything

do you have satisfactory sex

i mean do you like it when you have it

do you have enough of it

do you know how to love

do you love

are you loved

do you know how to hate

and do you

why do i prefer a disturbing theatre to a pleasing theatre tho
        i like to please

who are we where have we come from where are we going. gauguin.

who are the kings with diamonds in their eyes moping and mowing
        among our private shadows. barker.

must we love one another or die. auden.

what is the question. shakespeare. stein.

do you know that i have reached into my entrails and strewn them about
        the stage in the form of questions

do you know that i do not know what else to do

do you know that i need you that i am dying and will die
        without you

what is useful

what is a good question

what is a way to find answers

what will knock down the prison walls

what is the way

what is the relationship between the actor and the spectator

what is speech

what is the important inquiry

do we have time to ask all the questions

which ones do you want to ask

will you ask them now

what do we need

how can we get it

how can we touch one another

how can we make it happen

how can we make a theatre which makes love love now

how can we make a theatre which is worthy of the life of its
        spectators

how can we make a theatre when we do not know any answers but only
        have vague hints about how to ask questions

i end with questions because i have no answers

but what i want is answers

11

questions. 1968

how do we feed all the people

how do we stop all the wars

how do we open the doors of all the jails

how do we disintegrate the violence

how do we obliterate racism

how do we get rid of money (capitalism)

how do we undo early death

how do we end militarism

how do we put an end to authoritarian systems

how do we end the class system thing

how do we find the answers to these questions

how do we do it now?

12

Ai. Aieee. To get thru. Slash. Every day barbed wire, walls by the hour, unnatural barriers, prison world, everyone locked in geographically, economically, psychologically, locked in by class, by private property, by underprivilege, the society of doors, trapped in lower consciousness, locked in by knowledge and all its lies, locked in by the limits of knowledge and the lack of knowledge and all its airs, locked in by rivers, gravity, immigration officials . . .

Every day I am called to say Thou to my closest friends, and I am unequal to the task. Someone asks me a question but the effort is too great to wrench out the answer, and, helpless, a smile trembles on my face, I murmur something inadequate, and both of us die a little. I am locked in by what I am, what I have become, by what I will be if I don't get out.

And I am not starving. I am draped in privilege. Why am I suffering?

To get thru. To you. Our struggle is to dismantle the death machine. The death machine is capitalism. Our struggle is to open the doors of the world prison. The world prison is the social structure. Our struggle is to get thru to the possibility of being.

Nothing is more natural than change. That is what anarchism is about. Anarchism comes out of a simple recognition of that fact, just as the body changes from second to second, like the seasons, like the ages of man, like this planet from pre-history thru Marxian pre-history, history till now, on into the next development. Dinosaurs and dodos come and go, and we? The anarchist wants to create the conditions so that the process, this process of the universe, goes on with maximal effective extension of life and joy.

A principle of anarcho-communism: if you change the economy the mentality also changes; when we are living in community we will all be different.

The struggle: a voyage from places where there are books but no light to see, where there is food but no machinery to farm efficiently. My whole life has been a search for adequate means to process the food and thought so that we are adequately nourished, fruit.

A decade ago we were locked in, maximum security. This is a motion picture of a jail break, this life of the theatre.

The revolutionist walks on the edge of a knife. Buber.

My own life is marked by plays and actions, the life of the theatre is a process of going from one to another, half way along the path of life, in the dark forest lost, in the burning forest of the night, the furnace, the pit, the abyss, dancing it out.

This book is a movie ten years in the making. The process of breaking thru the barriers that blocked us ten years ago and how we are getting out and beyond is the code in which it is written.

The wandering body the wandering mind. The great gorgeous awful struggles which are our glory.

To get thru, to survive the tempest, to the continent, out of this death-in-life, to you.

Croissy-sur-Seine, France. 27 February 1970.

13

Three Meditations on Strategies.

One.

Breakdown of language equals breakdown of values, of modes of insight, of the sick rationale. Breakdown of language means invention of fresh forms of communication. Breakdown of language means breakdown of computers. Breakdown the language of the controlling forces and you breakdown their weary logic, you breakdown their tight structure. Shake things up, change, give ourselves over to what we do not comprehend, what we think we comprehend we don't comprehend anyway, our logic is false, is rigid and systematic, open it up. Breathe.

To free language (thought) from the confines of the Socratic rationale, which is now the strong weapon of enthroned imperialist democracy. We take language away from the governing class by subjecting it to the imagination, turbulence of the mind. Breton. What in the twenties was called the Revolution of the Word, but now we don't just confine it to literature. Free association, like the order of the future, as opposed to the regimental association of the societal structure that dominates body and spirit in our time.

Terminology like Kill the Pig: a paraphrase of Death to the Tyrant, the inverse of Long Life to the Czar.

The slave trade is now disguised. The length of the arrow. When the arrow is too long the shaft is broken. The percentage is indicated by numerals. The arrows fly with the wind. Calm. The mind is blowing from North East 20 percent. From W 1 percent. From S by SSE 18 percent. Paths by past years. Noontide. Terror.

Positions are shown, profits, the dotted blue lines show losses, approximations, considered tidal currents, approximations. Weak, variable, the solid shaft. Tidal ranges are large. The net of water. The influence of the continent. The arrows with solid shafts. The wandering mind drifts off this chart. Movement of water. Genitals, returns from which were obscured, scattered by the layers. Biologists do not fully understand the mechanism of the sound scattering swim bladder.

The search is now for a better way to locate targets. To sort the possible layers. To bring home samples, supplies, to avoid non-existent shoals, to measure the acoustic energy of the new language.

The layers themselves may someday be charted. When we have other instruments, free heads.

Until we never think of them, not with this head this Jewish mind, not with this ocean eye, this vessel confused instead, with tiny beeper crawlers, not with electric lines and readings, but with taperecorders and videotape because they can remember for us and we do not need all of it stored in the spinal fluid, not that the layers themselves won't someday be charted, they probably will be given favorable circumstances, free heads, but not with these words, not this poetry, but with the next way which may someday be the way to chart. I howl. But you, Achmed, you must stop brooding.

Where "O" is given, gales may occur and expose the futility of frail walks, lliana stalks. Don't brood about that. Proceed to next chakra, meditate, act.

Any wide departure from the normal pressure may reveal some disturbance and indicate a coming sweep after which no trace of depression could be found either in you or me, you who think you're so smart and half immortal, why do you know so little about navigational aid, constructive vitality? Drowning is not uncommon, especially in air. Suffocation. Work of our cooperating observers appreciated.

Very little change has occurred in frog frequency. Today there is a group. If you are interested in winds, blow your mind. On the side of the net, thrash new conclusions. Cut. New information is beginning to break. It began to unfold about twenty five years ago, but last July . . . it's beginning to break. Creatures are extremely delicate and have a high mortality rate. Do you not feel better already with wind in your head? Breathe, don't fail to breathe.

Rio de Janeiro. 20 October 1970.

Two.

Meditation on Action. 1967.

we are in great need of reality in our time

a generation rages: don't vote don't pay taxes defy the police burn your money puncture tires upheaval destroy the whole culture let go of the past shit on everything rather than the sterile power clean machine eat less wear less work less do nothing that does not contribute directly to great transformation poetry break every law to pieces break up the sidewalks walk on the earth find another life take your children out of school make flags into flour sacks destroy all government the wasting of time stop the time-clocks strike strike strike holy terror into our hearts reverse peristalsis drive out the money changers stampede the banks ban them the bombs and the whole thing of it dismantle stare dissolve grow fins fly focus feed exude light from the eyes beauty from the ears night exultation is one of the roads to salvation pound crack scream oggle wallow fuck creep crawl retch suck open the roof to the rain open the lungs the blood the cells to the plants high five fingered cannabis bright coca the languid poppy the secrets of the cactus the magic formulae of the earth are our chemical warfare against the killers recreate everything dislocate the brain which kills right and left revoke the pitiless modern mind lengthen this list with all variety of action until every sentient being eats right and left breaks the love barrier and sheds his anger his sexual revenge sexual revenge on everything

lick it all

begin again

düsseldorf to hamburg parma to perugia. march 1967.

Three.

i accuse   the   institutions and the structure
and of much bad   repression
of forcing   the imagination to go   into   hiding
of thereby creating much   frustration   such
frustration   that   the   world   cancer waxes greatly.
i   accuse   us
of   enacting   revolutions
                                                                which
feed   all   the   people
                              but
which   make us slaves   of industrial   tec
hnocracy   which cater to unnecessary material   impulses
and do not   see   need
seen   in   ancient proverb:
bread   is   not
                                                               enough
the total revolution: of   desire and need.

there is no time for argument. we must feed all the people
immediately and make sure that we are   not
inaugurating   a   plan in which   the mind dries.

porto alegre to são paulo, brazil. 13-14 february 1971.

14

Pause and begin again. Patchen.

BREATHING:

Notes for Lesson One

"When insufficiently supplied with oxygen, the nervous tissue and especially the cells of the higher divisions of the central nervous system

cease functioning." K. M. Bykov, "Textbook of Physiology," Foreign Languages Publishing House, Moscow, 1960.

The rigid position, unbending, in which we hold the spine and rib cage: the military posture of a proud and stiff-necked people: bulging chest, narrow waist, artificially maintained by sucking the stomach muscles in and holding the breath, fatally.

How the air enters the trachea, then moves into the bronchial passages. How we fail to inhale sufficient air to fill the rest of the lungs. How, consequently, there is not sufficient oxygen to nourish the cells properly. How the body chokes. How the brain rots.

How we are afraid to take a breath. How we are trapped in rigidity and fear. Afraid to move a muscle, the diaphragm. How we have to train ourselves to dare to breathe. Prana Yoga. Exercises in filling the lungs, in increasing consciousness of the physical apparatus, in using consciousness to overcome the results of the psycho-physical repression.

Breathing: something the revolutionary can utilize that cannot be recuperated by the governing forces: because it begins to lift the mind out of the lower regions, uprising, it releases imagination, understanding, vision, hope, ingenuity, spirit, strength, physical power, it extends longevity, it is masculine and feminine, this breathing in and out, it reduces sexual inhibition, and the liberated consciousness that follows is useless to the authorities who want us to remain rigid, scared, stupid, running.

Ritual: sanctification of the body: the repetition of certain prescribed actions in order to heighten deepen widen comprehension of the sacred essence: to make holiness conscious: to make of breathing a conscious ritual: to not let go of the life force.

On meditation: a combination of exalted physical consciousness and intensified awareness: while the body rests, carefully breathing, nourishing and cleaning the cells so that they can function productively, the mind travels beyond the limits set by the masters of our misfortunes.

15

Meditation. 1966.

Emergency! the horsemen riding down on us! we consume ourselves!
emaciation! we touch each other and off go the bombs, plague, plague,
the starving legs that cannot dance, the swollen bellies, the infants,the
folded hopes, the sack of the people, wiped out all their lives by our
systems, the system is plague, help, help, I cry out to you but you are
in your hiding corner, I cry out to you and I see in your frightened eyes
that you think I bring you mad hardship, the plague of battle, the
plague of change, I am the apocalyptic madman, the plague in its final
stages, epidemic of despair, thick fetid air, dying, we glance at the
mirror, decayed flesh, and we know we will die unloved and unloving,
the plague of the inability to express the love we feel, the terrible
plague knot of unexpressible love hardening like a stone in my loins
until I can hardly drag myself out into the streets, paralysis, plague, the
unexpressed flesh eating itself cancer, hide, shut up, turn off the lights,
police, enemies, targets, war plague, the torture instruments of imperialism, infested sores, plutocracy, dynasties, power plagues, water plagues,
plagues of factories, emergency, emergency, plagues of complacency, of
complicity, of aristocratic manners, plagues of cleanliness, shit, placebo
theatre, poison theatre, submarine mallets, assault by party banter,
enameled intellect, plague on the black man, exploitation, condescension, reprehension, debility, debacle, poverty, blunder, it is the plague
of selfishness, the people separated, bagged, heads in hoods, necks
roped, led, dragged, bumping, stumbling for a lifetime till we fall down
forever, starved, shot, corroded, too young, dead in bed from plague
exhaustion, once supple now cracking, unfinished, warped, like old
planks, unused, splintered, dead. Misery!

We know all this.

This is daily life. That we do not see it and cannot see it as we are: that
is why it is an emergency.

We apply the word emergency to times when it speeds up. We are in
such a time.

We know all this but we do not feel it. That is why 1966 the only
theatre is the theatre of emergency.

Whatever I do I am now a doctor. I have taken my degree in recognition of things as they are.

I see the gorgeous landscape, the light of the sun, I feel the impulse to love, I see the architectural splendor of Venice, I have studied Euclid and read the Propositions, the sonnets, the mystical accomplishments of Chassidim, the excellence of Chinese calligraphy, and screens, the arcs of bridges, the audio visual accomplishments of Carpaccio, the gamelan, the Parthenon, the colors, I have listened with attention to the languages of men, gazed on Mexican skin, Jewish breasts, I have licked every part of man and woman, I have explored in the Sierra Nevada, I saw the spot where Aeschylus split the rock into words, rain, rainbow, snow in Sweden, the Atlantic, the sea, destiny, glass, crafts, masses, processions, customs, costumes, acrobats, movies, inventions, ships, I recognize all glories, beauty does not escape me, I am always alert, I measure freedom wherever I am, the length of a field a person can walk, how far one can think, how far we can go with body games.

I see all the danger, the dissolution, I am not content, I recognize the emergency in every house and place.

1966. It is not what we do not know but what we do not feel.

The Theatre of Emergency is the theatre of feeling.

For a feelingless society, feeling.

For a fractured people, unification.

Realization. The people as one, one.

A theatre not for people, but at one with people.

Mending the gap between human nature and the human mind. Stein. We know what class hatred and race hatred are, but we can't get ourselves to really do anything beyond petty liberal gestures because we don't really feel what we believe. To change the world.

The theatre of change. Of emergency. Of feeling.

When we feel, we will feel the emergency: when we feel the emergency, we will act: when we act, we will change the world.

A theatre of action.

My vocation is the theatre, my life is in the world, therefore a theatre of world action. Art is not a profession but a path toward truth both for maker and spectator. Ajit Mookerjee, *Tantra Art*.

You cannot separate anymore. That way is over. The plague of separation. You cannot speak of change and remain unchanged. Therefore what you indicate on the stage you must live. Otherwise it's all invalid. The plague of lies. Art as anti-lie.

That may be the only valid function left for it in this emergency.

The theatre of emergency, feeling, change, action undoes the lie that spectators are dead by proving them active. The spectator becomes performer, the theatre becomes life, the emergency is the truth.

Taormina, Sicily. 13 March 1966.

16

To Bring Down the Structure. Police Theatre I

If we are going to bring down the structure, we are going to have to attack it from all sides, all ten thousand.

For the police: plays that increase doubt, that show order without law, plays that raise class consciousness, sexual plays, sexual crisis, *prise sexuelle*, plays that come in ten thousand shapes. The project is called Biting Thru. Without arousing savage reaction formations, the play that ultimately releases them of their authority.

Not to drag them like sharks from the sea to die stranded on the sand, nor to terrify them with sensations of castration, but the play that ultimately releases them of their authority, evoking holy instincts, the play that translates sadistic chemistry into human flesh.

17

Being vertical, rising upwards, homo erectus: this act of standing up, rising, is an act of defiance of nature: rising out of the depths of the natural into the supra-natural.

The work of the world is the shaping of nature, to resolve the problems of being which are submitted to humankind by the universe. And not to bow down, not to submit to the hierarchy of the elements, of scarcity, of death, not to be the abject subject of nature's oppression, violence.

The work of the world is the transformation of natural energy, violent when it is in its natural state, when it is over and on top of life, creative when humankind becomes creator. Prone, each of us is victim, inhabitant of the nether world, a cave dweller; upright, we zoom into the light, defying the oppressive shadow weight, we fly out.

18

When the sexual energy of the people is liberated they will break the chains. When the imagination of the people is liberated, they, not the artist nor leader nor spokesman, will find the way and will make it work. When the soul of the people is demystified, they will act with a power that far exceeds all technocracy. The artist does not have to blueprint the future. The people give the sign. Only a mass action can do what has to be done. That is strategically the most important discovery of our time. It indicates what the work of art is. The socialists and communists who have been proclaiming this for half a century have twisted it to mean that the artist should create things to support the bureaucratic state. The nature of the master is to lie.

19

There are always petty busts, followed by petty court scenes. A rehearsal of *The Maids* in Paris in our hotel room, October 1964. It's a beat hotel, Hotel Normandie, Rue de la Huchette, the manager takes fourteen francs from me, seven francs a day per person, every morning as I come downstairs. I have to go to Berlin, Judith is rehearsing with Bill Shari, Luke Theodore and Tom Lillard. The manager knocks, *"Madame, Violation de domicile! Vous ne pouvez pas rester dans la chambre avec des inconnus sans que votre mari soit présent! Si ces messieurs ne quittent pas la chambre tout de suite, je serai contraint d'appeler la police!"* No one leaves, so he calls the police, and everyone gets arrested. Several hours later, after being slapped around and beaten up, they are released. Opposite the *gendarmerie* is the Hong Kong bar, of which Genet speaks in *The Maids* when Monsieur, just released from jail, phones Madame.

We want to go to eat in Stockholm after the performance. But all restaurants are closed in Stockholm after 9:00 P.M. In fact Chester Kallman had warned us about this on the eve of our departure. He said, "Be careful, you cannot get anything to eat in Stockholm after 9:00 at night." We found, however, that there is one restaurant open there at night, the *Röde Rummet*, and it is for people who work at night. In the December cold we stood in line waiting to get in. (It is our habit to eat after performances.) Finally it was our turn. "You can't come in here," says the manager. "But we work, we work in the theatre," we explain. "No, you can't come in here." We refuse to leave. So he calls the police. Who arrive swinging. They grab us by the throats, that's the Swedish technique, and drag us away. We did not get out of jail until the next evening.

In Rotterdam we made reservations in the hotel and when we got there the manager didn't have the rooms he had said he had so we left, and he said "You are too dirty for my hotel, get out anyway." So we left, and someone swiped a towel, so he called the police, who arrested us all. The towel was returned but the hotel manager didn't want the police to let us go, he wanted to prosecute to the full extent of the law, and it took the tears of several women at the police station to get him off our backs.

In Trieste in a *tableau vivant* during the *Mysteries* an actor stood nude, motionless in the light, his beautiful sexual organs gleaming before 2,000 eyes in the fleeting 3 seconds of light. The *tableaux vivants* consist of 72 flashes: the lights go on: there are 4 people in 4 positions in front of 4 boxes: lights off again for 4 seconds, on again for 3 seconds, and the 4 people are in 4 different positions, lights off, lights on, lights off lights on. And someone 'thought' they saw a naked man, so they called the police, who charged into the theatre, and tried to break up the show, and we just continued, because who the fuck are they, and we did our play, and they arrested us after the show, and wouldn't let it go on the next night. And these are some of our many busts.

The bourgeoisie have things so arranged that they can call the police just about any time they feel like it.

The police are their servants. Read Strindberg: the servants find ways to dominate the decadent masters. They come on like vampires. But they still stay in Strindberg's house of horrors. Servants identify with the masters. Genet. That is their problem.

The police are not our servants. The police are not the servants of the people, but of the privileged classes. They are our brothers but they do not know it and neither do we.

20

The big swatter. The big drowner. Who drowns us in his own liquids. The big conductor. The big dividers. The big owners. Their stolen blood. Wings. They are beating on my back. What can I do? I open the door. I let them enter. Poor me. I sold myself. I have become a thing. Marx. And they, the big drowners, have us. We have also our big paranoia with which to devise theatres against them, the big takers.

The theatre as ceremony for exorcism of demons. Practical. Because when the ceremony is over the participants act the big people.

Gautama cut off his own eyelids when his awareness fell asleep. This planet has eyes and eyelids. When you don't want to take action you don't want to breathe.

Rome. June 1967. Cefalù, Sicily. April 1968.

37

21

Police Theatre II.

Smashed full in the mouth by his right(ist) fist, the hand of the free bourgeoisie: the policeman's fist. This is France, but let me remember Irak where last week they hanged fourteen dope smugglers! Let me remember thy glory, O Lord, and the glory of man, and the smirch of our bungling, the immoral lapses, the holes into which life falls like a hanged man. The Police State. They can hold you in this country for twelve days for nothing, for nothing, for "identity checks," for "investigation": more than three or four people standing in a group on the street (or in the Metro) constitute an assembly and can be arrested for participating in an illegal demonstration. Thus in France the masses cannot speak; yet the bourgeoisie—and even the poor—have been indoctrinated into believing that France is free. But we see you for what you are, you are subtle neo-fascism, France, you and all your sisters.

Paris. 2 February 1970. The story: the Metro rates go up again, 90% increase in two years! Who pays for this? Who gains?

A worker has gone to work on the Metro every day, back and forth, 12 times a week, 12 hours a week, 600 hours a year, 18,000 hours in the Metro in 30 years! How many in a lifetime? 700 twenty four hour days, 2 solid years in those subterranean vaults, 2 years of his/her life in the caves of the earth, the cave riders, the nether world!

Three days ago The Living Theatre Action Cell went out to the university at Vincennes to conduct a class. Conducting a class? Those days are over. So we say: Instead of exchanging ideas in the form of discussion (A Good Method for Drying Everything Up),let's use this time to create a play together. So we go at it.

1.) "We don't need plays, we need action." Agreed. "The people learn thru action." Agreed.

2.) What is the burning issue? Answer: "The rise in the metro rates."

3.) What is the goal? Is it that the people rise up and refuse to pay? Is it that the people flash out and realize that they are always being hustled by the system into doing things against their own advantage? Will the revolution start? What is the goal?

The goal is that the sleepers awake. The people are the sleepers.

Life is a dream. He only wakens who has set the world aside. The goal is to awaken the sleeping spirit of revolution, this is followed by morning light, revolutionary clarification and eventually (soon) by revolutionary action. Create unrest, a critical attitude. The first goal will have been reached when the people get started making preparations themselves.

Student: "You can't talk in this room because there are too many agents. All we can do is talk in generalities." "Then can we break up into cells and talk specifically?" Agreed. But it is clear to me that already it's out. The agents are surely here, as everywhere. POLICE STATE. The whole operation on Monday will be carefully observed and controlled. But we will learn from this.

The cells are formed. Each cell does its own work. The Living Theatre Action Cell does its own work. Its plan for the Metro Play: *Death by Metro*.

We work on it for two days. The piece lasts about forty seconds. If all goes well we could do it 20, 30 times in 20, 30 stations all day long Monday . . .

Then we plan the strategy. Pre-imagining all the possibilities.

Monday morning before doing *Death by Metro* two of us go to observe another group in action.

We stand in line buying tickets. 7 A.M. It is very clear that I am looking at faces I would never see inside a theatre.What right have I to presume that theatre is interesting to everyone?

It is interesting to those who have received the kind of conditioning that makes theatre interesting to them. The old theatre couldn't be of interest to these people tho. Why should they be interested in the passions of Faust or Phèdre? What the bourgeois intellectual aristocracy believes to be universal is universal only for itself, and yet the social structure would have us believe that no theatre can be created outside of its domain. It believes in itself as the ultimate Eden, a self-deception

39

that has been forcibly injected into the general consciousness. But the impertinence is disposed of by the dances and rituals of primitive societies. A different aesthetic is the answer. The aristocracy defined beauty in its own image. Sexuality is openly suppressed. Studies (Kinsey) of sexual habits in different classes imply that there is less foreplay when proletarians make love. They go right to the chakra center? They get it over with fast? They have not the disposition for it? They are too tired? The beauty that they see looks different, has different colors, the whole field of reference is something else?

"It may be that the civilizing process, the intellectual process and attainment, has brought us to the abysmal area of possibility in which we cannot experience God. Our civilization has made us godless people. You can't be civilized the way we are and believe in God." R. D. Laing.

What kind of theatre for the people who spend between 700 to a 1000 days of their lives in the tunnels? They . . .

We go to rendezvous #1, take Metro to rendezvous #2. Wait. We're spending too much time here. Nervous. To rendezvous #3.We we are waiting around too long. Comrades Q & R arrive. That's the signal. Q & R head towards the station cabin to take over the loudspeaker system. The others start giving out leaflets. The cops! Dispersal. Pierre B. and I move slowly so as not to look suspicious. After all, we're only observers "en passage." Cop grabs me by left elbow, swirls me around, blood of Beck stains peaceful demonstration.

That the people may know. All knowledge to the people.

"To put an end to the division of labor and of knowledge." Action Committee of the 13th Arrondissement, Political Programme adopted by the General Assembly of the 25th of May, 1968.

How can the masses transform themselves into something more than an amorphous mass?

"The ideas of the ruling class are in every epoch the ruling ideas: i.e., the class which is the ruling material force of society is at the same time the ruling intellectual force, the class which has the means of material production at its disposal has control at the same time over the means of mental production." Marx, cited by Daniel and Gabriel Cohn-Bendit.

"Hence one year of revolution gave the Russian proletariat the kind of education that years of parliamentary and trade union struggled failed to give the German proletariat." Rosa Luxembourg, cited by the Cohn-Bendits.

Twelve arrested. In the police wagon the cop who slugged me vomits insults all over us:

"You make me sorry I wasn't in the SS so that I could have really taken care of you and your kind. The people hate you! They don't want your bullshit! All you do is stir up trouble! That's why we have to take care of you!"

A young worker arrested with us answers back:

"That's why we have to take care of you!"

Big Fist: "You're too young to have your teeth broken. You're too young to have false teeth. It's harder to eat with false teeth."

Worker-Activist-Anarcho-Syndicalist: "There isn't too much to eat."

After four hours they let us go. Officially "twelve demonstrators were held for verification of identity," says the radio. That is the thin cover the French Police use for disrupting street threatre.

Guerrilla Theatre. Where? How? And there isn't much time.

Croissy-sur-Seine, France. 3 February 1970.

22

"The police traditionally hate French students, who they see as the pampered offspring of the bourgeoisie—indeed in their own Fascist way, they live out their part of the class struggle." Daniel and Gabriel Cohn-Bendit. *Le Gauchisme. (Obsolete Communism, the Left-Wing Alternative.)*

Police Theatre III.

They always make their own. Their very presence is the heightened moment. They are always in costume, even when they are in plain-clothes. In fact, in plainclothes they are really playing a role as we understand the term in classic theatre vocabulary: they assume a char-acter other than their own, they disguise themselves, put on the mask, mimic the habits and characteristics, and seek a setting, a background against which they can move in character. Charles Demmerle, a rightist, worked in the pay of the F.B.I. for about four years, cooperating with the activist left, even planting bombs—United Fruit Company, General Motors Building, Chase Manhattan Building, 69th Street Armory, in N.Y.C., 1969—those sensational bombings that jolted international equanimity. All the time disguised as a crazy leftist. And who then informed the F.B.I. so that the arrests* were made and the public satisfied. He played his play, the play of spy, stoolpigeon, provocateur, rightist, revenger.

What is interesting is that for four years his leftist friends were unable to shake him from his reality: they did not move him with the love force of their love, nor with the beauty of their belief, nor with the conviction of their passion, to cross the line, to play the play of traitor to his Police class, to revenge himself, and to become in fact what he was playing, to become a revolutionary. We do not know to what degree he actually helped in making and placing those bombs: perhaps he played a very special role, the role of schizophrenia which says, "Fuck you, terrorists, fuck you, bourgeoisie—(I bomb your crazy build-ings)—fuck you, police—(I aid leftists), and fuck mine eternal soul—I suck juices out of everyone!"

What does this teach us as performers. That you have to act everything with such conviction that the truth force and the love force and the life force are irresistible to all the other performers on the stage with us, so that we draw them into the magic ritual of turning the wheel and of restoring the earth to its joyous state of creative change.

The police are always in drama. And always playing the Heroic Protec-tor of the Ruling Class, whom even the Ruling Class dreads. (To the mind of the rich, prison is more fearful than to the poor, or to the revolutionary who at every hour has to expect it.) "Mr Antrobus is a very fine man, an excellent husband and father, a pillar of the church, and has all the best interests of the community at heart. Of course, every muscle goes tight every time he passes a policeman." Thornton Wilder.

Everytime we came to the doors of the theatre at the end of *Paradise Now* we found the police waiting to stop us from going out into the street. They made it clear that the enemy of freedom is manifest in the body of the policeman. To free the street: you can't: unless/until the power of police is destroyed, wilts, is transformed. How? This is what I mean when I talk about Police Theatre.

A scenario has to be written, a method must be found to get thru to the police so that they, like the soldiers, the army, can desert. Daydreams. Idle, useless. They understand life only in terms of cruelty, a formula which always ends with punishment.

The clue to the scenario: appeal to their dreams, their suppressed hopes, their real desires. (With hostility and stones we attack their consciousness, and thereby force them to fortify their defenses.) What we need is the invisible ray that goes around corners, a counter culture, penetrating the scrotum. Strategies for freeing the mind.

The object is to offer the police roles to play that surpass in pleasure the role of policeman. To create another play to gratify his ego and his longing cock.

* Sam Melville, chief among those arrested, was slain by the National Guard during the Attica Penitentiary uprising of September 1971, of which he was reputedly one of the chief organizers.

23

Police Theatre IV.

How to avoid the bloodbath when the forces of reaction come with their armies, their police? The beautiful nonviolent revolution? How?

Let us imagine the workers taking over a factory, and they go to the boss and they say, "This is the way it is now. If you want to join us join us, work with us, but not as a boss, as one of us, in the work of production, in joining the workers' council when the time comes—every six months or so we will form a new council of workers and we will make the decisions, and sooner or later everyone takes part in the council."

And the boss says, "No! The factory is not yours!" and calls the police (or the army or the navy). And the police come. But the police are, after all, the sons and daughters of the working class or the Lumpenproletariat, and they are themselves working class people, and for years the work of the revolution will make this clearer and clearer to them . . .

And the police arrive at the factory and the workers say, "Brothers, don't shoot us!" And the police reply, "Brothers!" and don't shoot . . . That's the nonviolent revolution.

24

The liberal says: "You cannot refuse dialogue with anyone, therefore you have to talk to me. In my theatre." Sophistry of liberalism.

Polemic. The liberals try to live on the border between two worlds, the world of reaction and the world of revolution. Naturally no one trusts them. What they weave in the day they unravel at night. Sometimes they'll put up the bail to get you out of jail. Sometimes they'll hide you when the cops are coming. Sometimes they'll pay the printer for the leaflets. They vote. They pay their taxes. They take mild action. They try to reform the system, but not to re-do it. They hope for slow transformation that will not disrupt their houses. Gradualism. When the revolution comes some liberals are going to fall one way, some others. Drawing the line time. The showdown. Making theatre for them has its uses but it will not bring about the revolution without which all the art and magic and philosophy and religion and all the sciences and all the technological advances will have been nothing more than the spastic failing impulses of an extinct monster planet.

25

Meditation. 1969.

this book being about
the role of the artist in the revolution:

it isn't enough to write poems to enlighten the intellectuals: for 400 years I labored under the deceptive theory that you could revolutionize the consciousness of the bourgeoisie or aristocracy thru the medium of art, and then they would transform the whole world . . .

The spiritual philosophers have been making the same mistake. The notion that knowledge, "high" art and "deep" thought exist only for privileged groups—and not for the people—negates/demeans the sense of art and science as holy beauty. How did we fail to see this?

Were we (the elite artists) duped the way the people are duped?

Capitalism and the State build grand theatres to contain the theatrical culture. At the same time art in such places liberates consciousness, the grip of the demons tightens.

What good are the complete works of Strindberg, Tolstoi, or Aeschylus if the spectator becomes simultaneously more and more bound in slavery to the system.

What good are the lyric orgasms if you have to pay for them with . . . your blood . . . your death . . . your soul on ice . . .

If you have to pay, who is the prostitute.

I am the prostitute, on speed, your fee pays me for my dope, sticks it up my ass. If I am a prostitute, you know what that makes you, Charlie. You think this can go on forever?

We, the players, are not going to put on those turkish indian mauves anymore to allure you into the scented safety palace. We declare the independence of the performer. Freedom from degradation for the worker-performer. Out of the fancy whore house jails. Into the streets.

The world. We abandon the harlots' arenas. Ah, the magic of harlots, the perversity of possession by masked masters. Oh, no.

— Performers' Liberation Committee.

What the next play is will be determined after we get out of the jeweled jail box, this Golden Prison. Prisoners do not know what they will do when they get out of jail. They only dream.

I am driven by the madness of my sanity.

For forty five years I have been trained to be an artist, to serve the culture in the capacity of artist. I am changing what was to have been destiny. They tell me I don't know how to make out there, on the street. We'll see about that.

For twenty five years a gorgeous courtesan. Now a street walker. We'll see about that.

The Theatre of Changes.

Vocation to be in the vanguard, along with the fools and the heroes, that's where ecstasy is, that's where I want to go, that's where I make out.

I like it where the action is. If it is useful . . .

I am always talking about feeding all the people. I who never feed anyone. Only stones.

Improvisations with the public tell me that not everyone is exhibitionist or extrovert (shyness has great beauty) but that everyone is a creative artist. Repression masks it.

The purpose of taking the theatre into the street is to smash repression. To disconnect art, artist and public (people) from the repressive arts of civilization, those arts that serve the repressive forms of society, strengthen them, and speak for them. Liberation is the word. No one is liberated who isn't free to eat.

Do I have a map? No. 1969. Wait a few years.

On the street, where the most important actor is probably Bread, the actor/artist/activist's superobjective is utility.

But I insist that it always be great art. Judith.

Great art means that you get swept, as if by wind (unseen forces) out of the solitary cells of the jails of suffering. Great art as the key for jailbreak. Great art not as creation but as key to creation. Great art means some kind of liberation.

Always the more beautiful answer for the more beautiful question. cummings.

How can the theatre help to feed all the people and not kill anyone?

Always the same beautiful question. 1969.

How do we rob death of its power? Gutkind.

How to effect the beautiful nonviolent anarchist revolution.

Always the same beautiful question.

Urbino, Italy. 22 November 1969.

26

Meditation on Acting and Anarchism.

The problem of the authoritarian position of the director. No function being more important than any other in the free society. Since all functions make the whole being. Am I alive without a finger. Without a heart.

The *Mysteries* had no director. We created it in less than four weeks, making changes from time to time during the following months. Some members of the company contributed more than others. What does that mean?

> "In a collective creation
> there are various contributions to be made
> Of different weight &
> of different importance:
> but that doesn't mean that they aren't all equal
> or that the work is not collective."
> Joe Chaikin
> *São Paulo. 9 August 1970.*

Judith and I still in governing position. Uncomfortable about it. We resign almost unnoticed. It's beautiful.

Frankenstein fluctuated more. Judith and Julian always charging first. When we flagged, others pushed harder. Total collaboration: direction scenario acting lighting setting costumes all elements.

The action is to evoke from one another the spirit of oneself, and in oneself to comprehend the genius of the others, and then to express this, communication.

The apotheotic moment at which a collective of individuals becomes itself. Where is the director? He/she is a glowing participant, no longer alienated from the performers, the performers from the director.

Frankenstein refused to cohere in the time allotted without the rigid schedules of the director.

Frankenstein threatened to engulf us. It did many times. The audiences in Venice and Berlin in '65, Cassis in '66, all applauded drowned men. We drowned and came back many times.

I got high in order to live.

Finally you can't get high, you don't want to go to sleep, fatigue takes over, the insane Mistral mistress, fatigue, the greatest high of all. Michaux.

In Reggio Emilia, working on *Frankenstein*, we cut all discussions.

We needed to control a project whose needs we could not measure. It commanded its own destiny. The directors, J & J, however, were building the spectacle for the talents of a company of performers everyone of whom they knew intimately. The performers directed themselves thru the medium of the director.

Northeim, Germany. 19 August 1966.

27

And then Mogador became unsafe and the whole world was unsafe, every minute unsafe. Then you work against that. Sometimes that means the creation of a new concept of being in order to survive.

It is a race. Examine the terrain on which the race is being run: sword blades, a little poppy seed, vermin, shadows, half the people behave as if they were buried up to the waist in cement, how can you get them to move. Steady boy, despair is not your game, it's always on the side of the loser. There is no guarantee of safety. Bastard death. Practice propitiation. Choose life. Wear shoes with silver wings. Race.

It is my luxury to speak of the race when my own daily chances both of survival and advantage are guaranteed me by the system. I will be protected, up to a certain point, by my class.

What do I do with this? What is guilt to me? I cannot live with it. Guilt is the Furies. My whole life, and yours, must be to appease them. The only possibility. When there are enough of us revolutionaries. We are trying to fix it so that by force of numbers finally comes a certain conscious act. It will follow a lead secreted by an expanding cellular structure.

Go at it from all sides.

I am separated from you and you from me until death, and no union. Why should it be otherwise? Of what advantage is it if there were no ravine between us? But you know the sadness in my beat-skipping heart. All separate. Wrong. All different, all individuals, but all relating to each other or dependent upon one another.

Without you I do not exist.

Proofs: Extreme punishment: to be separated from life. In Yemen homosexuals are executed by being thrown from a cliff. That's the ancient law. Nowadays they drop 'em from planes. In our time in California Caryl Chessman executed in gas chamber for committing "unnatural sex acts." Extreme punishment: solitary confinement.

The human being, even with our poor tongue-tied inappreciable meager expression, our failing attempts at communication, our total body of failure and failings, NEEDS the metaphysical presence, the nearness of other living beings. A dog. A cat. A bird. An ant. A rat. A man. A woman.

(The first thing about prison is being cut off from sex. Heterosexual experience is automatically cut off, and homosexual contacts are tracked down, ferreted out, forbidden, closely watched, caught, punished.)

I need you. You are my doctor, my healing agent.

Enemy is: absence of harmony: harmony is repressed by system: peace does not mean a world without conflict but without violence. Danilo Dolci. Life in harmony is not without conflicts, but resolutions always follow each other like the seasons, naturally.

Brescia. Italy. 24 October 1969.

More. Go at it from every side you know how.

Who grows my food, who picks my coffee bean, who makes music in my ear, who lays Atlantic cable, who cleans my sewer, who makes crowfoot civilization to invent the dream of community, who invents China, who Chinese language, who is shoemaker for my feet, who is arab ass for my lust. I depend on everyone.

Who depends on me?

Who am I to Peruvian wool carder, to Hong Kong woman who paints

50

the farting doll, to Japanese fisherman drying seaweed, to street sleeper in Bombay, to him with hoe in hills on rocky place. I suck their honey and pay them with enough rats to eat them alive. And what is my act of balance. The card is the Juggler. Play.

The landscape is a primitive train, built by British Railways late in 19th or early 20th century, Latin America, wretchedness. Babies, listless, doomed. The old sore women, the cold biting night, the strong urine, a clean people ground into dirt, the wooden benches and the train always lurches, the internal espionage, hunger. Ah, a man selling cheese sandwiches and ham, North American style feed, passes thru the corridor periodically, but no one has money to buy them. The train never stops, it is ceaseless night train to Mogador. Most danger is not worth it. This is.

Who presumes holy attitude? No blame. Only I say to myself: something hurts, what is it, and what can be done to heal it.

Who depends on me. I depend on everyone. How can I make the relationship reciprocal. What do I return to the textile worker? My art?

To the degree that the reciprocal relation between the parts is fulfilled: harmony, balance, ecological peace, and the organism which is our world is either in a state of creative expansion or of destructive disintegration.

Milan, Italy. 28 October 1969.

Without doctors, 1962, to pump the air out of my punctured lung (after being beaten up by cops during demonstration in Times Square protesting President Kennedy's decision to resume testing nuclear bombs in the atmosphere), I would not have survived. I depend on doctors. You are doctor? The planet dies. A suicide . . . When I am cut off from you. I affirm my great dependent love.

I am Hindoostan water carrier I am rice on back of Mexican burro I am product of Libyan dates I am Russian Intolerance I am American Pride I am Islamic Repression I am oasis I am actor and spectator.

I work in the theatre to open doors to the granary, I sharpen awareness,

I cut the curtains, the curtains of deception, beautiful, so that we can go thru together where no one can go thru alone.

Milan. 31 October 1969.

Going at it from every angle.

It is the theatre of escape. From death.

The vampires suck away at our energy and devotion until we are useless: I foresee the Museum of Planet Earth which the explorers from another galaxy one day discover and visit as we study Yucatan or the Nile Empires.

Milan. 1 November 1969.

The past has always to be opposed by the present. The continual struggle for liberation from the past brings the new life of time future. In order to perpetuate itself, that is, in order to stay alive, life has to change.

Clinging—cling not to the wave—to the past is necrophilia, it breeds corruption, death. It is sterile love affair, it is insecurity, it always perpetuates death.

And now, late century, things happening faster, faster, more people, more consciousness per thousand, more chemists, physicists, engineers, poets, visionaries and revolutionaries per thousand, more ideas per thousand, more piercing of envelope which surrounds us, Whitehead, more opposition, more rigidity. Gotta move fast. We are.

But not fast enough. Doom visions loom. The North American Indians saw the end of their civilization, their people. And they danced out their Vision of Death and Resurrection, they did the Ghost Dance on the Great Plains, in the snow, blanket wrapped, cold and despairing, they danced out a vision of annihilation of the White Man and of the reappearance of the Noble Savage and of their herds of buffalo, their red and black and yellow maize. And we see also the gleaming of something else, like our truncated souls rising up and running free, with the plenty and the beauty of the place and all the spiritual splendor that like amputated limbs clutters the landscape now. Is the leg of the chair you are sitting on the leg of the woodcutter who chopped it down?

I repeat: if we could feel, then we would feel the pain and the pain would be so great that we would end it. Artaud. We are mad because we suppress our feelings, that is why Mogador became unsafe.

End separation. End the pain.

This leads to anarchism.

Milan. 1 November 1969.

28

"Revolutions come like a thief in the night. They are produced by the force of things. They prepare themselves for a long time in the depths of the instinctive conscience of the popular masses—then they burst, often apparently touched off by futile causes." Bakunin.

29

Nomads live shorter lives but the wide range of their experience is their compensation.

In and out of theatres, packing and unpacking the cars, in and out of hotels, snow, rain, ice, no central base, it is like being a postman, a caravan, a supply route. And in a time when Chauvinism grips the people it is a life-bestowing pleasure to cross borders, even tho the customs men have begun to go thru our pockets and assholes and bindings of books looking for something Subversive. Tho they are wrong they are right because I want to subvert this jail. But my breath grows short and my muscles go tight, and I tremble and use up my fear glands. They take away an hour or two of my life just searching, but they are taking years, and as my resentment towards them builds, irrepressible resentment, they are taking still more time off my life. They are condemning me to death a little earlier. Because of the changes they put me thru. That is what border guards do. Nationalism is one of the first things to go after the dawn, comrades.

They really don't want any men with long hair traveling from one place to another. Some countries, like Mexico, won't let you in with long hair at all, some countries, like Morocco, try to make you cut your hair at the border. And they hunt for literature: Anything with the word "anarchism," whether or not it's sold in the stores of the country you're trying to enter, gets them going. They suppose they can stop the mind from breathing and expanding, they're flipping out.

But the sacred body of the human being is not the property of the state, nor of real-estate. I was born on this planet, it is all ours, on this planet I was born, not in this or that country; immigration laws, visas, passports, artificial lines, possession and control, all these belong to the nether world, world of thinghood.

World Government is World Illusion. War will become civil war, one president will rule with the strength now allotted to 150, the Law will remain all-glorious, all the demons, property, money, police, identity papers, passports and inspection officials will serve as security checks.

I propose to use the theatre to decrease the dependence of the ego of both citizen and police on nationalism, born of the possessive perversion, sadistic. I propose to use the theatre as a force for disseminating experience of the cosmos, driving our dead thoughts into the universe like withered leaves to quicken a new birth.

I propose to use the theatre to end the separation, to destroy the perverse barriers of land possession that divide our earth, our mother, and prevent the uninterrupted interflow of food and I and Thou.

Croissy-sur-Seine, Rio de Janeiro, Ouro Preto.
10 March 1970-21 May 1971.

30

Notes toward a Statement on Anarchism and Theatre:

The purpose of the theatre is to serve the needs of the people.
        The people have no servants. The people serve themselves.
The people need revolution, to change the world, life itself.
        Because the way we are living is too full of pain
        and dissatisfaction. Fatally painful for too many people.
        For all of us.
This is a period of emergency. Therefore emergency theatre is
        the theatre of awareness.
The first thing is to feed everybody, to stop the violence, and
        free us all. This is what anarchism means in our time.
The theatre of anarchism is the theatre of action.
The slavery to money has to end. Which means that the entire
        money system has to end. A society of free goods, freely
        produced, freely distributed. You take what you need, you give
        what you can. The world is yours to love and work for. No state,
        no police, no money, no barter, no borders, no property. Time
        and disposition to seek good, seek one another, to take trips
        deep into the mind, and to feel, to find out what it is to have
        a body, and to begin to use and make joy with it.
The theatre has to work with the people to destroy the systems of
        civilization that prohibit the development of body and brain.
        In order to work in most factories you have to stop the mind
        from working lest it die of pain and injury. You have to stop
        the body from feeling lest it wince consciously thru the day.
This is the work of the theatre.
Theatre has to stop being a product bought and paid for by the
        bourgeoisie. The whole age of buying and selling has to end.
        Theatre has to stop being the servant of a system in which the
        only people who go to the theatre are those who can pay for it.
The poor are disinherited. Well, activist artists are going to
        play in the streets,
we are going to tell what's going on, how bad it is,
and what the people can do to change things,
and what the destination—the objective of the revolution—is,
and ways to get there:

how to make the revolution, to bring it into being, and what to
        do when we have it, and how to carry it further.
The revolutionary artist will seek ways to drench the people in
        such beauty that they tear down the flags and subvert the armies,
        form communes and cells and a society in which there is a
        possibility of being.
Because bourgeois society doesn't tell the people what beauty is.
        The secrets have been appropriated by the rich with their
        exclusive education and avidity, and the people are poisoned
        by the mercury in the mass media.
The working people are going to take over the means of production,
        occupy the places of industry and turn them all into factories
        of food clothing shelter heat love and the extended mind.
It is going to happen.
And we are going to do this by exorcising all violence, and the cause
        of violence, the need for violence, violence in all its forms,
        violence of hands, teeth, bombs, police, army, state, law, land,
        real estate, property, education, social, political,
        moral and sexual.
This is the work of the world.
And this work of the world is the only work of the theatre:
because the theatre principally is the dancing place of the
        people
and therefore the dancing place of the gods who dance in ecstasy
        only amid the people
And therefore we aim this theatre at God
and the people
who are the destination of the most holy
holy holy revolution

Avignon, France. 7 June 1968.

56

31

Acting Exercises: Notes for a Primary Lesson (1).

Not to submit to an acting lesson unless its graphic purpose is clear. The body, if not stimulated by an inspiring impetus, does not react with interest. The movements, consequently the expression, are empty because they are empty of meaning.

The Living Theatre works something like this: we find an idea that we want to express physically. Then we do what is necessary to realize it. If it requires special exercises, then we do them.

Whenever we work physically we find things that we never could find if we did nothing but think.

We have rarely been able to find sufficient time simply to exercise. There is hardly enough time to do the necessary. Emergency.

All the time knowing that without living physically the powers of the mind diminish.

Therefore we are always individually doing Yoga, as we go thru the day doing other things we check our breathing, our posture, our movement, regularly. And the body's awareness of what's around it, and the space.

To train the body to extend its ordinary capacities. To extend imagination and intellect. Exercise should not be used to train the body to express the banal. We want things not yet known to the controlled consciousness which is ruining us. If sensitivity is not heightened by the exercise, and only the banal is expressed, we remain what we are, frustrated, unfulfilled, crippled.

Aimless exercise reinforces the accessibility of the banal.

At the same time it is important to nourish the body with use. The body understands that; but exercise without objective confuses the mind.

Acting Exercises: Notes for a Primary Lesson (2).

Joe Chaikin:

"There are two kinds of Groups:

"1.   Encounter:
to discover, challenge, know one another,
for this goal there is never an end,
there is never an end to know and struggle with each other.

"2.   A Task Group:
a collaboration:
to effect, penetrate, build, create
something.

This group requires rapport
but it is almost unrelated
to the rapport sought by
the first group.

"Rapport: if we look at each other intensely
or hold each other closely
or touch in the manner of love
that does not mean that we will have rapport.

"What will do it:
is something else.

"A distinction between aims:
some groups are psychological and some groups
have as a definite objective:
to create something.

"Improvisation has its own requirements
independent of you.
Unless you steer,
you are driven.

"Exercise:
You make a path
where there is no path
and this path

"is good for nothing
else except
to get you where you are going.
Never before and never again.

"It is the principle of invention:
The Unique Way.
First the aim:
you find the way to get there:

"That's it. The Try.
Unique. Never before and
Never Again.
The Principle of Invention."

São Paulo, Brazil. 9 August 1970.

32

Body.

The body gets further confined to thinghood in the outmoded theatre of our time. We have to revolt because we're fighting for our lives. In the outmoded theatre, sitting motionless and silent in the dark, the process-of-atrophy intensifies.

The theatre of the next development in human beings must direct itself towards the creation of conditions in which the public can experience its own physical self, examine its being, its own physical being, its own holy body, individually and collectively.

"Every authentic body can be nothing but a depository of holiness. Only what is pure can be made into body. The body is an ethical being, not an 'enemy' (the pure is *Kaschar*—that which is focused).

The impure body cannot endure; it decays. It has a semblance of life because the impure can partly devour the pure and thus assert itself for a while." Gutkind, *The Absolute Collective.*

Artaud saw in the famous beauty of oriental theatre a movement that made his imagination envious. But Artaud was hung up on IMAGES, the great taboo of the Jews who in transcendent understanding know that the seduction of the eye is so strong and pervasive that it threatens to be the undoing of man, and, Artaud, himself yearning for the Great Liberation, did not yet know as we do thirty or so years later, that the eye is not the major perceptor of the body. The Theatre Beyond the Eye. The Theatre of the Body That Not Only Sees But . . . . The Moving Theatre. Watch out. Move.

To observe only and not to act: to be reduced to less than life: naturally the linear reading society would tend this way. It is time to move on.

The Dionysian Theatre that leads the people into dance, wild hunting (we'll call it moving thru the world in search of what we deserve), and fucking, hints at what we are aiming at. But now we have not only to refer back to this suggestion out of human history, but to go thru it and find its double: other facets of body theatre, holy touch and use. But it is hard to talk about what we do not know. The lost continent, the body, another galaxy.

I have the courage to voyage because I have received messages about what my own body is yearning for. I get them forty times a day. Gleams. Glimpses. But fleeting. Therefore this new kind of theatre in which the actors and the spectators dissolve in each other, into the collective creation.

Physical. The lost body rediscovered. The body numbed by the industrial society. The body clamped shut by capitalistic morality, the body screwed by poverty. The body liberated by the food and poetry of revolutions. The body alive in action.

As if in the course of this play we confront the social problem which is haunting the community in the post revolutionary world: How to get out of this envelope that is encasing us and into the next. Flowing with the process, life always extending. Swimming, the sensation of being beauty, holy. Abysmal fluctuation.

Naked bodies in this theatre which is the world moving feeling beyond good and evil beyond metaphor beyond life and death "what is death?"

is a stupid question   to the body of the woman
in the   third   class   carriage   whose
listless baby's   body   has had no   food
for   three days.   Give
her all your money, weep, but the woman   and death
never   go   away   until   the
body
gets   its   due: Revolution.

33

Break down the resistances both of spectator and performer, essential of Grotowski's theory. Above all the resistance to change? Above all.

When the whole process compounds and conspires against us. Does not the collective unconscious accept the present reign, the patriarchy? Are we not transfixed by family, business, law, with all the preconceived values, as if they were eternal? Eternal for us because we shall die before they are altered. Now, that which is alive changes: that which is inorganic, stone, can only be changed, it cannot change itself. Remains fixed: resistance to alchemy. Process, in which the imaginable (which is limited) is possible, in which the imagined (which is possible) is dismissed as impossible out of resistance to change rather than out of a valid sense of reality (knowledge of what is possible). Extending imagination, the first function of poetry. Poetry as magic potion: the spectators imagine the unimagined (resistance number one gone), feel desire all over their bodies (resistance number two), accept hope—discard despair—(resistance number three), are captivated by the soul of action (resistance number four), lift their hands (resistance number five), break the chains.

34

The performer is always in a state of trance.

The trance state of the performer.

This is true in the conventional theatre, in dance, in jazz, rock, opera, music hall, all the forms. This is true in the street when it is street theatre, in demonstrations and confrontations. This is true of the revolutionist making the revolution.

The method of Stanislavski is a *pratique* to induce trance. Just as a participant in primitive rituals receives the spirit of another being, and then assumes his character, so Stanislavski formulated an elaborate theory of technique to enable the actor—with rational processes of accumulative thought, empathy, sensation, recall, study, observation, physical and psychological identification—to assume the identity and characteristics of someone else, mystical, fictional, usually the creation of the imagination of a writer. Then the performer reaches the point at which she/he "lives the part." This is rationally induced trance.

Any act of confronting the public automatically induces trance because the body chemistry changes. To meet the needs of the situation supraordinary powers are commandeered. One "loses" control, a mysterious control controls, it is a force which is not the ordinary self in its ordinary state, other aspects of the performer's personality are activated, you become another you, if only because a more rarely expressed facet of the self, which exists, now controls. The meaning of trance: consciousness without consciousness, a state in which often enough you are "possessed" by another being. In the classic theatre, the performer is "possessed" by Elektra, sometimes we even say *is* Elektra. In the rites of possession, in Brazil, the mediums are possessed by spirits and demons, and they then become the medium of expression for them: physically, spiritually, vocally, they take on the gestures, and often put on the costumes and use accoutrements designating the very specific spirits or demons by whom they are possessed. They are in trance *because* they are possessed, as by a *Dybbuk*.

In acting political theatre for example, aided by the performer's state of trance, I am rendered capable of talking to the public directly (with love), whether it is the oppressed or the dominating class. Ordinarily I am not equipped to do this. Because I am "not" myself, I can communicate with people whom I cannot contact when I am in my usual sealed-off, alienated, inhibited state. Hip language would speak of my performer's high. When high you can fly over barriers, some barriers.

That's why I act, that's why I get high. Because it is a way out of the narrow confines of my own social class.

When the people play the Theatre of the Revolution they will be tranced out, they will act propelled by the Spirit of the Revolution, possessed by the Creator Spirit, as they fly out of the narrow confines of their own social classes.

Rio de Janeiro. 11 November 1970.

35

Reflections on performances:

Paradise Now: Anger and violence. Passion, rather. The ravings and raging often carry the performer to a level of poetry and creativity, the unleashing of forces that know the passwords that open sealed passages, the creation of psychic changes that penetrate the armor of the mind.

More than anything the performance is a trip, a state of being. The change that came with *The Brig* (1963): fiction seen as a parenthesis in the history of art: the end of enactment. In performing *Paradise Now* the actor confronts himself. Both the highest and the lowest levels. Trying all the possibilities to get thru.

I am trying at the same time to get thru to myself. I am pressing up against a mirror. I don't get thru. I don't want to get to the other side of the mirror. I want to get thru to myself. I'm pressing against my own image. No good. Nothing works. I want to get thru to you.

I am talking about acting forms.

I shout because you cannot hear, I am screaming, it's the collective scream of the suffering and the angry, I am a medium for the rage of the mute oppressed. I am crying out before you trying to get thru: scream! Something is happening, the shattering of placidity. Louder! I'm beginning to hear you. The juices are flowing. Fertilization.

Beware the rational. Betrays us all the time. The rational kings with metal in their minds, the rational generals putting shrapnel in our groins, the rational corporate conference table bloated with laborers dead of fragmentation torture, the sucked out bodies of the banana pickers who nourish capital and the state. Rational. Calm. There is nothing to be calm about tonight.

I rage: flailing my arms: metaphysical semaphore: I am performing: tantrum, flipout, flashout, agony, wail, insult, tirade, old techniques borrowed from Seneca and Racine, I am out of my mind, at last I am glowing, coal-like, heat emanates: I will burn my way into you: this is my act.

Lear and Krimhild had relatively nothing to be angry about. The landless peasant has something to be angry about. There is much to be angry about. Shall the people be denied the death struggle of great drama—the mad scenes, the tirades, the reconciliation, the rapture? We are talking now about a theatre of anger, anger as the expression of real feeling.

What is the difference between the violence of starvation and the violence of screaming at someone about it? In *Paradise Now* we learned not to confuse the violence of the cool impersonal people with good manners who exploit ... strangle ... starve the starving ... and the violence of those who scream. Still we said, "It is the system, not the men."

The performer has to find those forms that break thru, that disarm us: it's desperate: we have to get thru. The great art of I and Thou.

I am a lover and this is my passion.

The *Mysteries:* Paris 1964, we were no longer playing characters, but ourselves. In the ceremonies of possession in Brazil, in the rituals of *Umbanda*, the mediums are possessed for instance by the spirits of the "*Pretos Velhos*," the old black slaves. The bodies of the mediums contort in violent spasms, the spirit of an "Old Black" enters them, and they, stooped, grunting with lumbago, bent over from hard labor, express the character of the old slaves by whom they are possessed; but the spirits of the old slaves give them miraculous powers: great wisdom, the power to answer questions and to give efficacious advice, wisdom transcending the cultural wisdom of the white colonizers. Here the "acting" of character transcends its "more refined" theatrical counterpart. In the refined theatrical counterpart the performer speaks only the wisdom written by the great poet who was possessed by the Creator Spirit when writing. But the event is one stop removed from life. It is the unreal world.

Stanislavski's obsession with realism, with the illusion of the real, was all part of an attempt to recuperate the power of this reality. The importance of reality is clearer to the tribal Africans in their ritual than it is to the performers in the old theatre, who, after all, in their daily lives, far from the soil and the production of the necessities of life, were already in the world of the unreal.

Now we are moving rapidly closer to a civilization in which technology, population, science, the hoodwinks of repression, are going to take us further and further from the reality of the nourishing and productive earth. The ritual, in which mediums are possessed by attributes other than their own, may be a means of holding onto the reality which is being driven out of existence. The *Mysteries* taught us the pleasure just of being ourselves. The performers, like most people, have been afraid to be themselves. Until now.

The Establishment dreads the revelation of reality and wishes people to be things other than they are. Marx. The *Mysteries* revealed, the *Mysteries* opened the door to a subversive technique: the courage not to be cast in a role.

Frankenstein: the Theatre of Character is over: it was clear in Act II when we played the legendary figures of the Greek Myths (Daedalus, Pasiphae, Icarus, Ariadne, Theseus), when we played the life of Gautama and Yasodhara, or the Four Horsemen of the Apocalypse (War, Famine, Plague, and Death) that we were twisting ourselves into the dishonest world in which the mind and therefore the body accept the crushing myths of character. These myths, with all of their seductions, actually rob us of the universal experience because they stop us from being ourselves. We live in images.

Neither will the spectator wear a mask when he enters into action:

despite all the power and beauty of masks, ravishing deception, he will impersonate himself unmasked as lover or hero, as provider or inventor, as initiate or guide, possessed, yes, possessed by the Creator Spirit: so that the vines burst from our fingers, so that the grain spray from our seeds.

Iowa City (Iowa), Rio de Janeiro.
21 January 1969 — 11 October 1970.

36

Television. No matter how much information it supplies, it always makes the people weak, it takes away their power, it always makes them passive spectator, it never takes them to another life, another perception, dots and all, cool aspects and all, it diminishes awareness, it always says: I am the great machine, the miracular transporter of images thru the air, I am magic and you therefore believe in me (because magic depends on belief). I am strong and you are weak, I am power and you are flesh, I am intelligent and you are stupid, I speak and you listen, I am and you watch, I do not see you, I do not hear you, I do not care about you, I convert you into a sack to receive me, I convert you into a consumer society, consume my message, you are a thing that buys, you are a pouch for my insipid information, I do not want to touch you, I do not want to involve you, I want you to sit there, to be conditioned by your own passivity, go into debt to possess me, feel your weakness, feel my strength, worship me, desire me, be my slave.

Audience involvement as antidote for this, in which people don't just watch heroes and heroines acting it all out, but in which the people themselves take action and become heroic. Because the play/event only works—and the solution to what is otherwise a tragedy is only discovered—in the moment when the people are no longer the slaves of images parading before them, in the moment when they are instead possessed by the Creator Spirit and act out the creative impulses.

When the theatre by-passes the field of artificial fiction, the old system is short-circuited. Flash, shock, revelation. New conditions.

The museum kills art as experience by the behavior it demands of the visitor. Be tranquil, repressed, inexpressive, well-behaved, whisper, walk softly, respect the inner trip of the stranger, hold back, do not laugh with the madness and glory of what your senses perceive, hold it in, kill it.

Individuals don't need to desire money in order to perpetuate the money system. The abstract corporations do it. They beam control, they want the money. Prestige is the corporation and its symbol, the hideous signature, the trademark.

Many signs of death begin to appear . . . induced by technology, corporations, museums, televison.

Yet thru technology anarchism becomes all the more feasible. Democracy does not. In democracy, technology controls. In anarchism, technology serves. Because the people are aware. Democracy, by delegating power, underdevelops awareness.

Boston (Massachusetts), Granville (Ohio), Rio de Janeiro.
November 1968 — 11 October 1970.

37

Stars? Heroes and Hero Worship: leading roles/supporting roles: the cult of personality. And that is all there is to say about the Star System.

```
                        The galaxies
are     like     white     dots     painted     on     a balloon
rapidly being inflated.                      it    is    the    ex-
panding universe.                                              his-
torical evil         begins                      to disappear
when                                                    the
revolutionary's process         begins.         the process of
self                                            emancipation.
the     balloon     eventually     explodes           ? "they
say     the     sun     is     going     to     burn           out
```

67

in   two million years   and   the
earth's   going to freeze,
miss hayes," said one of my   8 yr. old classmates
in the third grade.   "That   doesn't   concern us;
we'll   all   be   dead,"
said miss hayes, and   the
whole   class laughed.
until   forty   years
ago   astronomers thought   that there   was
nothing   beyond our galaxy.
it   is   a   fabulous
voyage.

i go on to the next task not because i forget i am energy but because i
remember the voluptuous pleasure this fabulous voyage has to go on all
night forever but it will not unless we
calculate   how   to   keep   it
going
if   it   is   not   too   late.

In haiti   the   life   expectancy
is   38.   a hundred years
means   nothing to miss hayes.
don't imagine   that   the historic   process
moves   like   slow   slow   motion
and   that   you   will   be
dead
it   can be   hurried   if   you
like   revolution   more
than   airplanes   or
frigidaire evolution   two
useful objects   which
right now are   produced   by a
painful   system
we   find   ways
to   change   things
and   if   not
we   suffer
and   continue to   struggle
to change things: "the more you struggle,   the intenser
life is,   the more   fabulous
the voyage." kropotkin.   for

thousands of years we've worked on this poem. now it is life and we
work on it still.   the

suffering   does   not   stop   the beauty
and   the   beauty   does not
stop   the   suffering
It   answers   the   destruction.   rexroth.
the   suffering   flesh   the   overflowing   life
                              the   intenser the   struggle
the intenser   the   life.   intensity   intensity
as   compression/extension   of time.
the balloon   eventually   bursts
if   too   rigid

São Paulo, Brazil. 18 January 1971:

the situation here is critical, as it is everywhere. apocalyptic vision as
the year 2000 approaches. the life expectancy here is not too high.
birth rate is. in the sky emergency. in the ragged huts, in the military
belt, the strangle hold. in the rainbow swim, the rainbow effort, the
Rainbow Movement, approach of many colors. white light. dark countries, dark time, also time of beauty. beauty which enhances life but
does not halt the emergency, the rapid loss of blood. Bursting wounds,
bursting stars.

São Paulo. Brazil. 22 January 1971:

At the same time you try to live so that your life is poetry. This
generation realizes that the real work is not commerce, art, science, or
bastard love: it's to change it all: liberation: that's our vocation, our
fabulous voyage, starlike above the stars.

38

You can never tell performers to move to the right or to take a step
downstage. They have to be doing something. You can't give a performer just a technical direction. There has to be a motivation; it must be
more significant than getting out of the way or filling in the space.

Whatever the performers do, they have to be creating something or else they are wasting their lives. The state and capital are always telling the people to move over there and to fill in the space, their directions are not creative and none of the performers in the great world drama is not wasting his/her life. That is why we have to change the *mise-en-scène*.

Paris, Granville (Ohio). October 1967 — December 1968.

39

The heroic voyage of performers. How they get out of the labyrinth of lower consciousness.

And then, when the participants (misnamed the audience) all become the heroes and heroines in life that the performers intimated in their art, and when the performers take the heroic trip in life that they imply in their art . . . and the people . . . out of the labyrinth of art . . . up out of the vaults . . . air . . . life . . . it all begins to happen . . .

The voyage of performers into other characters: they demonstrate for the spectators the ability of the human being to understand people and events that are outside of themselves. We go to the theatre just to experience this, to listen to the person who hears the cry of the hungry, the sorrow of the people, black pain. The tuned-in performer whose muscles identify with the black writhing under the white feet, whose sensitized litmus soul reacts to black nausea and power, he/she is the beginning of proof that the battle of the peasant class and of the wretched of the ghetto can extend beyond class barriers. There is here the evidence that unification, the integration of the races, the gathering of diverse forces is possible: the secret of the performer's black art.

When we talk about arousing all the people so that they enter the theatre of life, as performers, acting great drama, we are seeking also the release that would make it possible for the white/the ruling/ race to comprehend the misery and splendor of the exploited people in the street, and to play it out in all its colors. The whites will eventually be coerced into this anyway by revolution from below. They must make an interior revolution. An historical problem is:

Questions 1971:

How can the ruling class make that interior revolution before the people rise up and act?

What position does this take in the order of priorities?

Paris, Rio de Janeiro, Ouro Preto. October 1967 — May 1971.

40

The Seven Imperatives of Contemporary Theatre:

1. In the Street: outside of the cultural and economic limitations of institutionalized theatre.

2. Free: Performances for the proletariat, the Lumpenproletariat, the poor, the poorest of the poor, without admission charge.

3. Open Participation: Break thru, Unification: Collective Creation.

4. Spontaneous Creation: Improvisation: Freedom.

5. Physical life: Body: Sexual Liberation.

6. Change: Increase of Conscious Awareness: Permanent Revolution: Unfixed (Flexible, Free) Ideology.

7. Acting as Action.

1970-71.

41

Scenery. Once upon a time it seemed to me very important. I spent years of my life nailed to it.

The Art of Stage Design. Using the eyes to heighten understanding. To visualize the secrets of the drama, to fascinate a thousand eyes with the mystery of the world of sight and sense, to send messages to the spectator, the word spectator used accurately. I trained by looking at the world, the perspective of cities, the harmony of all things, the ornaments, I collected mental images, kept an archive in my head, gathered odd pieces of wood, plastic trophies from the garbage dumps, and saved them in my studio for the right time, the right play. Every director has the perfect Chekhov table cloth waiting in his closet, said John Boyt.

I wanted to make sculptures in the stage space that the eye and actor could wander in, that the director could work on like a novelist moving characters around, that would shiver with splendor or crawl with vermin, which the spectator could use like a dreamer, the interdependency of things unfolding for him as image yields to image. It was my pleasure to do this work.

I worked slowly at the beginning and fast at the end.

I worked directly on the stage, relating to the space like a sculptor or painter. Many many times I would make something, or a whole set, and then take it down and start again, and often again and again and again, I would sit silent in the theatre staring at the stage, searching for the solution: how to make the set say what the play wanted it to say. The whole process made me crazy, glassy eyed, obsession engagement, I plunged into the work as into the ocean, then I swam for my life, sleeplessly for days, for weeks, sometimes for months, fatigue carried me along and provided its own invisible fuel, adrenalin, igniting ideas, faster and faster towards the end, the pressure of time and money pushing out my eyes, squeezing out the solutions, delirium, I let the terror demons chase me, I invented them, I invoked them, I raced, like Sacher-Masoch being whipped into glory, then the goddess, it was a pagan ritual, would enter, and the play would open. What did I know then about Death? He was not yet choosing partners in the play that I was in, I was young.

All the time the object was to avoid using money, to transform *objets-trouvés*—old lumber, paper kites, bicycle wheels, glass, auto parts, whatever—into something useful, at least to the extent that they became magical components of the decoration of the stage. Abandoned things became useful again. Resurrection. I believed that it was a real struggle for truth to smash the attitude of the commercial theatre which liked to dazzle its audiences with extravagances, not of imagination but of expenditure. In this way the public could be sure that it was getting its money's worth. I broke my body, pleasurably. So that the spectator could look at the stage and learn that it wasn't necessary to spend a lot of money to create the spectacle.

It would have been better to have . . .

There were always certain guides:

- a. If the set cannot tell the spectator something that a bare stage can do better, don't make it: superfluous ornamentation diverts concentration from the center, much of the manners and morals of middle class life are ornamentation designed to divert concentration from the center of things.
- b. Always make the set like a sculpture: make it on the stage so that the space relationships are solved by human touch.
- c. Avoid the artificial conventions of scenery: painted flats, backdrops.
- d. Decor is only interesting when it's the Double of what's happening.

It would have been better to have . . .

No more prettiness, only the beauty which can propel us out of the human condition.

It would have been better to have . . .

We have to work with poverty of means, because it is with poverty of means that we must confront the established forces, we are going to make them fall with ingenuity and inventiveness, with our superior intelligence, and our convincing beauty.

It would have been better to have . . . not practiced illusion.

73

42

Ramakrishna: If a man acts as a servant of God, he will hurt no one.

But we have to stop acting like servants.

Meister Eckhart. Plotinus. Traherne: It is as natural for a man to love as the sun to shine. Niebuhr talks about moral man in an immoral society.

"Man" here is a generic term referring to some kind of "ideal." The term really does not mean the people, just as it scarcely even includes women.

"Man" makes the society. If it is immoral, Niebuhr, "man" has permitted it to fall that way. Moral man is aware man. He must know when he is permitting his world to decay. Morality without awareness of everyday reality is abstract, nothing.

Holiness, God, the soul, love, peace, good: as if—if everybody got very holy—it would be possible to solve all our problems. But people cannot have holy relationships with one another when all relationships are servant-master relationships. Money means forced labor.

In the pyramidal structure in which we dwell everyone either serves or is served, except the lowest who are not served by anyone and the highest who do not serve anyone. Except God: therefore the notion of serving Him (masculine) has been elaborated.

It is hard to be holy when sexual control is creating anger, violence, and corrupt sensations. It is hard to be holy boxed in by laws which limit thought and action. ("Possession is nine tenths of the law.") The ceaseless propaganda of capital and the state warp psychology and condition all thought processes.

What can be done? The spiritual revolution will always be corrupted by the regime unless the regime undergoes revolutionary changes at the same time that the spiritual revolution is happening. Simultaneously. The two simply have to go on at the same time.

Lenin says, "We want the (Socialist) revolution with human nature as it is now." This statement, urgent, compelling, a nerve center of all of

Lenin's thought: we must concentrate on the political/social revolution first; the spiritual (moral) change, character change, follows later.

But, Vladimir Ilyich, what is there to prevent the two from happening at the same time? The exterior/anarchist/communist revolution and the interior/spiritual/sexual revolution. We must examine every revolutionary precept in the context of our own times.

In our time, this is, in fact, already beginning to happen. The political activist revolution is being surrounded by moral consideration. The life-style-psychedelic-love-people are, without doctrine, on the verge of politicization. Watch.

The people will never fully trust any revolution until nothing is left out. The people know that life includes all the elements. So does the revolutionist.

Air London to Paris. 27 March 1970.

43

Letter on Revolution. Judith Malina to Carl Einhorn.

Croissy-sur-Seine
Sat Mar. 28. 70.

My dear Carl,

Just returning this minute from London & really the first minute I've had to write to you . . . I want to get all the chores out of the way & start the real work. I have not yet read the mimeographed tract you said was important—though I've looked at it—I will study it carefully, but till then I know that while this is the direction our people are taking we cannot rest, we cannot stop, we cannot speak of anything but changing the situation.

. . . We *must* bring hope & *concrete plans* & useful proposals for feeding the people that do not entail the enslavement of the people by small cliques with guns and bombs.

Please draw up *NOW* your most practical proposals & order them into a readable form —

We must get together our most constructive ideas: And if we have none—then we must begin with the reality that we have none.

It's not enough to set up "communications" between "revolutionaries" who have no revolutionary proposals except . . . the road to the same old authoritarian world.

We have to bring sensible alternatives to people . . . *of course* we will "work with what there is" & WE WILL ALSO CREATE WHAT THERE "ISN'T YET" & "WHAT HAS NEVER BEEN" (THE OLD FORMULAS ARE STALE & DEAD) & "WHAT IS RELEVANT." But it's only "relevant" if it leads to something more human for the people & the proletariat than to dream of becoming "dictators" as in "the dictatorship of the proletariat."

I talk to everyone and ask what they think can be done & everyone comes up against the same wall & draws a blank.

A useful plan to which people can turn with hope which will bring energy —

I am convinced that this is the only valid work —

We must raise a standard that can show the way. It must be economically sound, humanly practical, taking into account human failings & human behavior, it cannot be a Utopian dream—but must be explicable step by step. You said that in the old American and French Revolutions no one had a platform—but look what happened! The American Revolution led to Amerika, & the French to Napoleon's coronation as Emperor—and the Russian, which planned for "the interim socialist step" that you have such faith in, led to Stalin —

Let us speak of Cuba and China — but let us speak of what will happen *after* Castro & Mao—is there a system there that can survive the death of the great "philosopher-king," that ideal Platonic ruler which these two men in their wisdom & talent represent?

We can make excuses for history, or say things have changed but we can't dismiss all its lessons. As Patrick Henry would say:

"Jesus had his Paul, & Lenin had his Stalin, and Mao & Castro . . . ('Treason, treason!') . . . can profit by their example."

Make the best of it.

We need a new form.

There are better people than me to find it.

But they are not doing the job. And it must be done. Hillel: "And if not I, who? And if not now, when? And if I am not for myself, who shall be for me?"

I will follow anyone who makes the destination clear—but if no one does it—I will ask them to listen to me & I will make it clear—or else I will expose the weaknesses of every ideology now going—will destroy the illusions & leave only what is real—human, meaningful, practical, & beautiful.

And to those who say it can't be done I'll say bullshit & prove otherwise.

What side are you on?

I'm on the side of those who believe you when you say:

1 plus 2   or   2 plus 1

"(1) Stop all the Killing ⇆ (2) Feed all the People."

The Maoists have the second part right but are very fucked up in part 1.

The Pacifists are right on the first part but don't know how to accomplish either part effectively.

And if you switch clauses, or the order of the clauses, as you want to, my dear Carl, you don't really solve, you put off—and maybe that's the best you think you can do.

But I'm on the side that can do better.

Que Faire? Let's find a way to make it work.

A comradely embrace and sisterly love
ALL POWER TO THE PEOPLE!
TO ARM IS TO HARM!
THERE ARE STRONGER FORCES
THAN GUNS
TO MAKE A NEW WORLD!
FIND THEM!
LOVE
Judith

The forsythia is brilliant yellow behind the house, a cherry tree blossoms across the road—but Brecht said, "We live in an age when to speak of trees is almost a crime." Love.

Postscript: I have now read carefully the little manifesto of the Detroit Workers' group. You are right, it is interesting. We must pay the closest attention to these tendencies. There are several important points the writer brings up. The emotional appeal in the description of the strategic vulnerability of the cities, or of the paean to the validity of valorous "close-quarter combat" is undeniable. But such arousal is pseudo-political. For example, if close-quarter combat means bayonetting a man in the guts, to speak of this "with great joy" seems to me questionable. But the writer's rhetoric covers that: I begin to see the uses of that weird jargon "glorious People's Army," or as this tract says "People's War of National *Salvation* . . ." There's a way of twisting the values semantically—because the author's thought it through—and his reader hasn't—and this jargon takes advantage of any intellectual vulnerability, or the deadening effects of social conditioning's deprivation –

I'm speaking of the intellectual starvation of the poor—their hungry seeking striving minds still gobble up hungrily what is presented to them—and this jargon is the sugar-coating!

We must scrape off all the artificial coloring, whether it be red, or black, or gold & look at what it means: "the party commands the gun . . .," the author's linking of anarchism & nihilism with "guerrillaism" (which its friends call 'Guevaraism"), the description of the control-state of Army/Party which gives a grim glimmer of the author's Post-Revolutionary World. He quickly follows this down description with a rousing piece about the vulnerable cities & this quickly gets the blood boiling with a description of the US bourgeoisie . . .

Good craftsmanship—this is not the work of a committee—this is a very clever person. And a person who speaks for a growing tendency—who says rightly: "We must smash the revisionist line of 'all politics, no warfare,' & the opportunist line of 'all warfare, no politics.' "

But I add: "We must smash the 'State made of the bodies of Armed Men.' " We are getting ready. I wish we could talk.

Judith

44

The urgent work:

A Joyous Proposal for a Nonviolent Anarchist Revolution.
A Practical Proposal: How To Make It Work: How Nonviolent Anarchist Communism Functions.
A Compendium of Technical Formulae and Data Supporting, Validating and Encouraging the Joyous and Practical Proposals.

A Variety of Techniques for disseminating this information among the
   people.
A cellular network, cadres, to carry out these techniques, and to do
   whatever necessary groundwork is called for by the Proposals.

The people will do the rest.
We will all become the people.

Cefalù, Sicily. March 1968.

45

Improvisation is related to honesty and honesty is related to freedom
and freedom is related to food.

Improvisation: Some precursors:

1912:	Duchamps: *Objets trouvés*
1916:	Arp: Collage of Pieces of Paper Arranged According to the Laws of Chance
1924:	Breton: *1st Surrealist Manifesto:* the principle of automatic composition
1942:	New York School of Action Painting
1952:	John Cage: *Music of Changes*
1962:	Allan Kaprow: Happenings

Pirandello's *Tonight We Improvise:* The first time The Living Theatre
did this play was in 1955, twenty five years after it had been written.
There was little in the play that was really improvised; Pirandello wrote
all of the 'improvisations'; but it was set up and directed so that the
spectators often imagined that it was really being improvised. William
Carlos Williams' *Many Loves* fooled around with the same kind of
tricks. So did Jack Gelber in both *The Connection* and *The Apple.*

Historically: While we were playing these plays in repertory we flashed
on what was happening. We resented lying to the audience. Honesty.

We weren't really improvising. There were occasional moments in the free atmosphere of Judith's *mise-on-scène* for *The Connection* that left room for the performers to move around and throw in remarks now and then, especially during the jazz sections when the performers could in fact move freely.

Jazz. Jazz is the hero, jazz which made an early break into actual improvisation. It was related to the automatic writing of surrealism. Chronologically the improvisatory flights of jazz musicians antedated the experiments of Dada and Surrealism. We listened to Charlie Parker stunned: he was pushing jazz improvisation far out. He was creating in our ears. Like David Tudor playing the Music of Changes. He inspired us, he showed us that by becoming really engaged and then letting go the great flight of the bird could happen.

With *The Brig* came The Living Theatre's first important art-of-acting discovery. Kenneth Brown had written a play in which the action was bound by rules, but within those rules only improvisation was possible. He provided a situation in which improvisation was essential. It was real.

The actors in *The Brig* reported that something special was happening out there, on stage, in the "cage," something which didn't happen in other plays. All the years that performers had been talking about re-inventing each moment, (the whole stack of evidence and exercises compiled by Stanislavski and his school), we had been fooling ourselves. Make it real: the real trip, physical, invented from moment to moment, reality, reality which is always changing and creating itself, the need for reality (life) in this period of alienation; improvisation as the breath that made reality live on the stage. It would never again be possible for us not to improvise. We would have to construct plays with forms loose enough so that we could continue to find out how to create life rather than merely repeat it.

Inch by inch, step by step, thru the labyrinth towards reality. The *Mysteries*, 1964: (1) improvisation within fixed limits (as in *The Brig*) (2) exercises in freeing the body and the voice (the organization of expression) from the limitations of the ideas contained by language.

Improvisation, reality, freedom: had something to do with eating: in those days (1963-64) we used to harangue in the streets at peace rallies, "Every six seconds someone dies of starvation and this is ECONOMIC VIOLENCE"; but we did not connect it closely enough yet with the work of the artist in his voyage to discover freedom, and now, 1970, someone is dying of starvation every two to three seconds and the repression is growing every second, and the art is getting freer. But is it?

Laborious voyage. The process of realization has been too slow. Does the establishment know there is this subversive relation between improvisation and freedom and the distribution of food? Does this account for the barriers to understanding that have blocked this voyage toward the truth so long?

You cannot be free if you are contained within a fiction. Reality has been wiped out; we are living the myth of ourselves: we have to create reality.

The revolutionary pursuit of freedom, freedom of expression, freedom of body, freedom of possibility: these freedoms are the freedoms sought by the intellectuals. Genet says that they come after other freedoms: after there is freedom from physical oppression, like the freedom the blacks in the U.S.A. and other places are after now. Order of priorities, he calls it. And of course, he is right. Feed All the People comes first. Stop All the Killing comes first.

Is there any connection between the struggle for freedom from physical oppression and the struggle for freedom from sexual and intellectual oppression? If so, what? Reality: the urge, primal, in all life, to experience life free: because we know instinctively that it is in freedom that life flourishes, finding the means to preserve and further itself.

Passing thru screens, over walls, slipping past the guard, so that it was possible in 1964, I note the passage of time, what moves and from where to where, how it is doing arithmetic, multiplying and dividing, history teaches, learning increases, perception furthers, and in 1964 we finally came to Free Theatre for the first time, it was the concluding piece in the *Mysteries*.

Free Theatre: no rules, no end. It ends when everyone has gone, when everyone feels like ending it.

But at that time, 1964, we felt insecure playing Free Theatre.

We preferred to end the *Mysteries* with the Plague, and the next time we did Free Theatre was in Milan, in June 1966.

Free Theatre means that anybody can do anything he wants to do. It means that "anything that anyone does is perfect."

We were asked to do something for a special benefit performance for an Italian theatre magazine, *Sipario*. We could do anything we wanted to do, pieces from *Mysteries*, whatever.

Judith suggested our doing Free Theatre. She wrote a few words to be distributed among the public so that they would know what was going on.

The mimeographed piece of paper that was handed out read:

FREE THEATRE

This is Free Theatre. Free Theatre is invented by the actors as they play it. Free Theatre has never been rehearsed. We have tried Free Theatre. Sometimes it fails. Nothing is ever the same.

The Living Theatre

The benefit took place at a party in the Palazzo Durini where there is a small and elegant theatre. The party was acid rock, un-political, and Babylon.

Free Theatre: When the time came for us to begin we gathered on the stage. None of the guests paid much attention. The stage was crowded with them anyway. We stood there. We absorbed the vibrations and absorbed the situation. Meditation on everything. Each one of us was looking for the most precisely relevant thing to do. Without speaking to each other, we formed a tight nucleus with our bodies. Silence. We got very close together and did not move and did not speak. John Cage taught us to hear the silence, Wagner played with silences too but that was drama, Cage's silences are metaphysics and sonic research. The intensity grew. The Italian eye sees everything a little bit like a potential photograph in a scandal magazine; they looked at us that way, the close proximity of cunts and lips, cocks and fingers in that body pile. The guests got heavy, then angry. "Do something!" they screamed.

They began to push, poke, grope, they began to play Free Theatre. They found our answer to their hysteria unbearable. Our response was motionless and silent. They got angrier, they began to fight. The police were on their way, we knew it, we split, the police arrived.

The next time we did Free Theatre was in *Paradise Now*. It was clear from the beginning that Free Theatre would have to be an integral part of the *Paradise* structure. But "how" remained obscure until very late in the whole process of constructing the play.

It would not be possible to do a play called *Paradise Now* and not (1) be free, (2) free anyone who might not be free. (To the point, alas, at which you draw the line or at which the line, alas, is drawn.)

To bring this about: in *Paradise Now* we called into action mysterious forces: the influence of color, the wisdom of the *Book of Changes*, the physical-spiritual journey of Kundalini, the arousal of the energy which rests in the chakras, the holy world vision of the Chassidim, the high vision of the *Kabbala*, we energized the body segment by segment, and we devised rituals, movements, sounds, visions, and cadences that carried the actors (the guides) and the public into trance. In trance, in a spaced-out condition, maybe we could enter Free Theatre.

Paradise Now was a voyage into freer forms, until, high, we walked into the street and re-entered the World Prison.

Free Theatre is illuminated by its failures. Where there is freedom failure is tolerable and takes on other qualities, and the joy of being free—"Do nothing, Do anything. Be."—sustained everything.

But the situation in *Paradise Now* was hermetic, just because it was inside a theatre—with or without paid admission—the life of money threatened each one each second, because the police were always in the theatre and the army outside, and the maintenance worker in the cellar.

Free Theatre: ultimately free theatre is improvisation unchained.

Free Theatre: a situation in which performers and public get the taste of freedom . . .

Free Theatre: free action: there is no Free Theatre until we are no longer prisoners in the world . . .

Eventually Free theatre is dependent on our playing it out in life ...

Free Theatre: no money ...

Free Theatre as secret weapon of militant artist ...

46

Collective creation: The first Paris *Mysteries*, October 1964, was our first experience with the process. It happened naturally, without effort.

All our subsequent experiences were long grinding efforts.

In Paris we were almost not aware quite of what we were doing. We stumbled into it.

Later we recognized it.

"Whenever I paint something there's always an image; sometimes I know what it is, sometimes I don't." William Baziotes.

A mysterious force, something simply stronger than our conscious intentions was at work. This mysterious force created a logical and controlled work.

Judith titled the evening *Mysteries and Smaller Pieces*. At that moment the meaning came a little clearer.

We had created mysteries without knowing what they were. We had made our first experiment in collective creation without knowing it. The way of working felt organic.

Collective creation.

A group of people comes together. There is no author to rest on who wrests the creative impulse from you. Destruction of the superstructure of the mind. Then reality comes. We sit around for months talking, absorbing, discarding, making an atmosphere in which we not only inspire each other but in which each one feels free to say whatever she or he wants to say. Big swamp jungle, a landscape of concepts, souls, sounds, movements, theories, fronds of poetry, wildness, wilderness, wandering. Then you gather and arrange. In the process a form will present itself. The person who talks least may be the one who inspires the one who talks the most. At the end no one knows who was really responsible for what, the individual ego drifts into darkness, everyone has satisfaction, everyone has greater personal satisfaction than the satisfaction of the lonely 'I.' Once you feel this—the process of artistic creation in collectivity—return to the old order seems like retrogression.

Collective creation is an example of Anarcho-Communist Autogestive Process which is of more value to the people than a play. Collective creation as secret weapon of the people.

In collective you create both thru yourself and thru others: inter-inspiration. Superflash.

At the same time, the process is tedious, it is boring, it is hard work. You have to go thru boredom. The boredom, the difficulty, are the lever. Create the boredom. Create the difficulty. We create a room in which we get ourselves so crazy that we have to find the door, the way out. This is one technique.

To experience boredom so intensely that you come out of it somewhere else. Cage.

Boredom, degradation, oppression, monotony, deprivation: the masses are going thru the boredom now, the suffering.

To create an ambience which will lure inspiration. The Muse. It can also happen easily, as with the *Mysteries.* Or Kronstadt.

These are the techniques of the collective creation.

47

You cannot rely on inspiration. You cannot build a strategy for creation based on something so unreliable. Judith.

Ouro Preto, Brazil. 5 December 1970.

48

The chemistry of the body provides the substance for alchemical theatre. The alchemy is those mysterious changes, metabolic, electro-chemical, flow of blood, glandular, neurological.

Paradise Now: the search for alchemical formulae: in addition to incantations: scientific procedure: dialectic.

Crowley: *The Master Therion:*
> "There is no grace: there is no guilt:
> This is the Law: DO WHAT THOU WILT."

"The Magician should devise for himself a definite technique for destroying 'evil.' The essence of such a practice will consist in training the mind and body to confront things which cause fear, pain, disgust, shame, and the like. He must learn to endure them, then to become indifferent to them, then to analyze them until they give pleasure and instruction, and finally to appreciate them for their own sake, as aspects of truth. When this has been done, he should abandon them if they are really harmful in relation to health or comfort. E.g., one might have a liaison with an ugly old woman until one beheld and loved the star which she is; it would be too dangerous to overcome the distaste for dishonesty by forcing oneself to pick pockets. Love is a virtue: it grows stronger and purer and less selfish by applying it to what it loathes, but theft is a vice involving the slave-idea that one's neighbor is superior to oneself."

What magic, what alchemical changes, unexpected, unknown as yet to man, can produce a state of freedom in a society in which it is not possible for one of us to be free until we are all free?

In *Paradise Now* we looked for illogical catalysts with which to precipitate the age of freedom. We consulted the oracles, we used the arcs of our bodies, our lurching minds, incantation, raising and lowering body heat, breath, wind, human contact, patterns of light, spells, rituals, visions, dreams. The Double of what is called "magic," "the theatre of illusion": in which the impossible happens.

The changes necessary to transform and transport us into a state of well being (freedom—to be free is to be free to eat) have the quality of the impossible. Because freedom cannot yet be experienced in our world: we aim at it, as we aim at union with God, the All Mighty, the Eternal, the All, the All in Everything, the Singing, the Dancing.

Because we only have had intimations of how to precipitate this condition, I call the formula we arrived at in *Paradise Now* "magic" or "alchemy"; and it was our attempt (1968) to create an alchemical theatre. The theatre has always been called—and indeed always has been— a place of illusion. The degree to which the illusion of theatre becomes reality is the measure of its magic. The degree to which it changes body dross into energy is the measure of its alchemy.

Alchemical formulae, Revolution, that will turn the gold into bread, the iron of the heart into the irresistible flesh, and the apathetic minds of men and women (the mass) into energetic sources of invention.

49

"The old theatres are nothing but a seduction to bourgeois values." Judith, in conversation.

"Art is dispensable. The aim of art is to destroy the need for art, the aim of art is to abolish art." Piscator, quoted by Judith.

"Artists put their morality into their art. Art lovers do the same. Their standard in art is high. But they have no standard in life. In art they can differentiate between good and bad, between right and wrong, love and hate, in art they can distinguish what is holy, what is meaningful, and where the truth is at. In life they are cold and stupid." JM (Judith Malina) at rehearsal.

Enlightenment: the need for secular morality?

For me the bourgeoisie is always there, always, confronting me, because I am it, and in it, and of it, and know it, because it is mine, and I sing of it to itself. Because I am singing my way out with a knife.

The entire first part of my life, forty five years, was spent addressing the bourgeoisie. Now, middle class persons with intellectual longings can be convinced of the need to liberate the blacks and the children of the third world. They can become anarchists in principle, or Marxists, or Jeffersonian Democrats, and they can really come to believe, given enough evidence, that there ought to be no laws and no money and no police. You can break down their reservations. Intellectually they will do everything. They will do everything except get off the backs of the workers and the poor. What? Because power corrupts, material power corrupts. And the bourgeoisie will even be convinced by the beautiful action of revolution itself when they see it. They'll accept it, not fight it all the way, yield; but they will not overthrow the State, they will not relinquish capital, it's in their blood and brain by now. They can't do the necessary thing. And furthermore, and most importantly, they can't because they haven't the means to do it, they can't take over the means of production because they don't know how and haven't got access and they lag in impetus because they are afraid of losing what they have. They have the consciousness of a greedy culture, a greedy-making culture. Whereas the proletarian, and Lumpenproletarian, if moved to act, could do the necessary; they have the knowledge, they have access, they have nothing to lose but their chains.

The race right now is to arouse the people to action. Before the great opposing camp secures them with heavier chains or drugs or another carrot. Because the modern industrial state knows that a discontent proletariat won't do what it's supposed to do to keep the structure standing, the machine delivering its goods. So before the proletariat is robotized by all that bad food and watches and TV sets, before they fall asleep and wake to find themselves pod people, we have to get thru.

The theatre that addresses the bourgeoisie and denies itself to the people, the repressed masses of people who slave so that the bourgeoisie can buy their theatre tickets, betrays its often heart-felt intentions. Maybe that is one of the meanings in Artaud's call to "Burn the texts!"

In order that the bourgeoisie be able to share the pleasures of liberation from their own tragic existence, we create a theatre for the poverty stricken, who are not only denied food and freedom and culture: they are also denied the truth. This is what we aim at changing when we aim at creating theatre in the street. Tho the state and capital control the mind-bending mass media.

"What," says the Red and Black militant, when we say we want to try to create theatre for the workers, "you think you can get their attention? We can't get them to read a leaflet!"

"Comrade, the theatre begins by being attractive . . ."

Notes:

Mao Tsetung:

"Our enemies are all those in league with imperialism—the warlords, the bureaucrats, the *comprador* class, the big landlord class and the reactionary section of the intelligentsia attached to them. The leading force in our revolution is the industrial proletariat. Our closest friends are the entire semi-proletariat and petty bourgeoisie. As for the vacillating middle bourgeoisie, their right-wing may become our enemy and their left-wing may become our friend — but we must be constantly on our guard and not let them create confusion within our ranks."

("Analysis of the Classes in Chinese Society" (March 1926),
Selected Works, Vol. I, p. 19.)

"Whoever sides with the revolutionary people is a revolutionary. Whoever sides with imperialism, feudalism and bureaucrat-capitalism is a counter-revolutionary. Whoever sides with the revolutionary people in words only but acts otherwise is a revolutionary in speech. Whoever sides with the revolutionary people in deed as well as in word is a revolutionary in the full sense."

(Closing speech at the Second Session of the
First National Committee of the Chinese People's
Political Consultative Conference, June 23, 1950.)

Commentary: Opens the possibility of making the revolution to the widest spectrum possible.

Wilhelm Reich:

"Revolutionary politics, in its content and the language it uses, is either an expression of the primitive, uneducated, life-centered character of the broad masses, or it merely calls itself revolutionary, and is in effect reactionary and barren." (*What Is Class Consciousness?*)

Commentary: This book (this writing of mine, *The Life of the Theatre*) is it a seduction to bourgeois values, this appeal to the elite (in the language of the educated elite)? Do we cut ourselves off from the people when we speak to each other in such coded symbols? Is it in effect reactionary and barren?

It is in finding the answer to these questions that my life rises and sinks.

50

Can art transform the world?

THE ELEMENTS OF THE STORM

Begin:
    1.   The Thunder:
        The form and substance of art have been shaped by the ruling
        classes into something that is secret:
        THEY HAVE MADE ART INTO SECRET SYMBOLS
        which serve the few
            (being understood only by the few)
        they have made art the privilege of those who are the cul-
        tured few.

2. The Wind:
The culture is created by the means of production.
Therefore you cannot first change the culture and then the
means of production.
You have to change the means of production: i.e.
capitalism:
then
the culture will change.

3. The Clouds:
The artist who *talks* about
revolution
especially
about nonviolent revolution
is just blowing words:
(aesthetic) *masturbation:*
(To fuck takes also a certain kind of courage!)
Action is valid.

"The anarchist," says Marx speaking of Proudhon, "when he
doesn't have an idea, can always find a word."

4. The Static:
Keys. The manufacture of keys is the work of the artist.
Hiding the keys is the work of the jailers. Opening the
doors—only the people can open them.

Open the doors. Property is theft.

It is the jailers who are the thieves.

5. The Lightning:
Art for the people? The people whose monstrous efforts make
the light (the coal the oil turbines dynamos switches wires
installations), the lights that shine in the dark, the lights that
prophets and poets extol, are too tired to look.

Working in the mines nets the Brazilian worker the equivalent
of about $40.00 a month, in the U.S.A. a miner gets about
twenty times as much or more; both are doing work so painful, so hard, that it makes thinking impossible, forbids it. In
the factory people who think too much go crazy—or start a
forbidden revolt: revolution. Work in the mines, the foundry,

the factory, cuts off feeling: who could feel and not crack up? If you sell yourself (labor is sold) you become a thing and you feel nothing.

Those who contain within them the power do not know how to free it. The work of the theatre has to do with activating the people by restoring the ability to think and feel freely, distributing stimuli that will free their bodies, their imagination, and above all their power.

This is the holy terror up the sleeve.

Brescia (Italy), Saramenha (Brazil). 23 October 1969–3 June 1971.

AIR CURRENT

New forms. The police always expect history to repeat itself. Once you try a revolutionary tactic, they expect you to repeat it, so they take the necessary steps to repress it. Outwitting those who would withhold information from the people, that's our work, obviously that's why the idea of guerrilla theatre is so instantly appealing. Because it implies adaptability and mobility. Also courage, to which we all aspire in this society which separates body and spirit and makes cowards of us all. The guerrillas give courage to the depressed people. In order to give it they have to have it.

Actor's note: The essential preparation is finding the courage. Courage will then carry to the creation of plays and will make it possible to play them.

Paris. 22 February 1970.

"Now I seem to see it, clouding my vision . . ." Antigone.

CLOUDS

The running stream of repressive criticism:

a. "It is the function of art to present things solely for contemplation."
b. "The artist is neutral; the public must be 'free' to decide 'how' it thinks."

THE LOCKS OF THE APPROACHING STORM

What is presumptuous here is that art should address the public as if the public were free to formulate its own reactions. It presumes that the public becomes free by being cajoled into considering itself free. When in fact it is not.

Reactionary criticism: would like art to be beyond the "mundane preoccupations of economics." It would in fact like art not to be hot but cool, a stronghold of composure. It doesn't want art to lead, but just to be there, graciously decorating an otherwise sordid and difficult life, an ornament which dispenses inapplicable wisdom, which teaches, if one disposes oneself to learn, which never addresses the mass (dangerous), but only the isolated individual.

But art is throwing off its chains. I use the proverbial language because it is big and true. Art will not serve that in which it no longer believes. If it does, it is no longer art. No longer art because no longer true.

Art as truth. If the truth-vision of art moves the public to tearing down the courts of oppression, to occupying the industrial plants owned by the thieves of life and time, to burning down the structure and replacing it with free communities producing for our needs and giving all the opportunity to fulfill their desire, to tearing down the brain structure, and the physical structure of our own oppressed selves, instead of merely leaving us free in the golden prison of contemplation where we repose rotting, incompetent, and impotent: then it serves a function; otherwise it is minion to the ruling class which has always adored great contemplative art, tho it has resisted profound study—making profound study available only to the isolated hermits, philosophers, ecclesiasts, or aesthetes—because profound study would lead to a sense of truth which no ruler can hold onto and at the same time hold on to empire.

Art which does not lead to action: the cupbearer of oppression.

The power of art is the power of truth. The shrill cry of frightened scholars: "Do not exert influence! Let be!" But the truth is influential, it is powerful, it reaches the recesses of the mind. You cannot ask the truth not to exert its powers. The truth is one of the most important instruments in the people's struggle for food and freedom. We are out to exercise the occult powers of the truth. *Ahimsa*, the force of truth: who can resist it? How long?

Croissy-sur-Seine, France. 2 April 1970.

HAIL

Breton speaks of surrealism as mechanism for releasing imagination, which we know is cooped up, repressed, and so we can't even imagine the solution. We remain where we are, rotting. But haven't all artists always believed that their work increased the possibilities of opening the doors so that the imagination could dance out the solutions to our own misery? We see now thru the clouds that art cannot withstand alone the overwhelming onslaught of the culture created by a class system.

Croissy-sur-Seine, France. 2 May 1970.

WINDS

Art is evidence of spiritual content in daily life . . . Art reports it, but this content remains shut up, waiting to be released. JM.

Paris. 18 July 1970.

WINDS (SOUTH)

— "A revolution involves a change in structure; a change in style is not a revolution.

— "A revolution in poetry or painting or music is part of a total revolutionary pattern. (Modern) art is fundamentally subversive. Its thrust is toward an open-ended (continuous) revolution." Jerome Rothenberg/*Revolutionary Propositions.*

But it's not enough: without further revolutionary activity its "revolution" is no longer subversive. It's only a change in the metaphysics of the atmosphere. Other than that it helps the upper classes maintain their vantage.

— "The confrontation between poet & political revolutionary moves toward a showdown that the poet seems fated to lose. But their lasting union would signal a turning of history & the reconstitution of Man in Eden." J.R. *(op. cit.) Second Series.*

CLOUDS (CUMULUS)

"Le théatre est une révolte contre l'ordre établi." Jean Duvignaud.

Art is revolt. It is the revolt that fails.

CLOUDS

The critic is buying advisor for the supermarket of culture. He advises buyer and seller.

He separates artist from artist and weakens the gathering of the forces.

Criticism feeds on rivalry, is hooked on competition (the principle of capitalism), it is an anti-body in the communal society: because the critic alienates himself, sets himself apart, the criticism of our culture is divisive. Auto-criticism is unifying because it is neither homicidal nor suicidal.

CLOUDS (CUMULO NIMBUS)

You ask performers, artists, what they want to do, why they paint or work in the theatre today, 1971, and they answer: to increase communication.

Communication, if it means only communication within the already privileged classes, the intellectuals, the rich, and the little richies, is not communication, it is shut-off, it is increase of alienation.

THE CALM BEFORE THE STORM

Form:

Pierre Biner: "Form, ah form ... No, the book (*Procès du Festival d'Avignon, supermarché de la culture* by Jean-Jacques Lebel) will not be very sensational. There are already three hundred books on the events of Mai '68, and those who read such books will look at it, but the people are tired of the form."

That's it, even the revolutionaries tire of the form. But the people with whom we are trying to communicate thru the media of the demonstration and the confrontation, the on-lookers, how much more quickly they tire, because they are just looking.

Novelty. Modern painters found the means of giving heightened perceptual experience to the middle class intellectual and to the rich by constantly re-inventing styles.

"The environment changes demanding change in form in order to communicate." Ernst Fischer. Now, we have to find new forms for revolutionary action to do this. We do not yet know the magic love zap that will transform the demonic forces into the celestial. But we know that it will have a different form.

THUNDER AND LIGHTNING

The spectators who are devoted to capitalism fight the revolutionary hydra of light by admiring its form and subtly ignoring the real beauty: that aspect of the hydra which is frightening and resplendent. They lock it in the experimental art box and decorate their houses with it.

Part of the solution then must be the action, the holy rite we can perform to break down their resistance against change.

This is the abyss. It strips the old wills. The body wishes to function differently, it rearranges its construction, the nervous system applies itself to new functions, the imagination which made fire, language, medicine, will choose other ways to live in the world, to communicate, to cure, even to choose. To liberate the imagination of the people . . .

That is why the performer is not seeking enactment but states of being that invite imitation. Aristotle. The character without underwear, without the attributes of social history, is the new revolutionary being whose world is based on human needs: bread, beauty, wisdom, love, unity.

For ten thousand years we have been living in not enough, everything is not enough, everything we do. We can't do more until we increase our capacities to do more. To increase the capacity of the people to become the people. Then they dance round the altar, naked, nourished, expanding like hope, creating from its own wreck (Shelley) the thing it contemplates.

When this happens, then the revolution, Messiah, will come, because we want it, and, wanting it, we will have to create it.

Rome. 8 February 1968.

THE LAST BLUE ON THE HORIZON

I used to get turned on by Mozart and Vermeer. Twenty years ago. I don't anymore. There's something wrong with that sunlight. Those pearls. Those elipses of the mind. That taste of tragic blood. I know that that can't be everything.

The privileged people get a dose of Mozart, and it's so beautiful that they begin to think, "Now we have to get everybody to have Mozart. Manufacture transistors, taperecorders, disques by the millions!" All that is happening is that Mozart becomes either consumer-item or status-item, and supports the reactionary principle.

Total assault on the culture. Ed Sanders. Burn the texts. Artaud.

Does the total revolution seek bridges back and forth in time? After the revolution time will be different.

I don't need to read Racine now, tho the study of Plotinus, the civilization created by the Vandals, the fossils of Africa, or the songs of the dead Navajo, or European Bakunin, may still enliven my life and work. Reading: what is reading for?

Latin me that, my linear scholar, out of your capitalism into all anarchy. Out of paternalism into maternity. Out of the battles and races of sexes into the new non-aryan eras.

We who want to burn the texts and read them too. The Tree of Knowledge and the Tree of Life.

From those who took the trip so long ago, whose ideas and words now are soiled by fact, whose light is leaning low, who lived for us, I take the light of the *Kabbala*, of Boehme, of Epictetus, of that warped politician Seneca, the illuminations of the *Tao Te King*, I take the light and pull at the rays as if they were elastic bands to see if they extend their light in the darkness of our days. So that we can find our way out of here.

Poisoned light? From the land of the dead? Seeping into us?

Reaching across time to enlighten the present (and to perpetuate what is dead) we catch the disease which the old light spreads as it spreads?

Would the light of the bonfire be more useful?

And tho I still read in the old books, I can imagine that interest in books waning. I find it hard to look at painting anymore. Images. That form of art is over for me, and even the birds of so much poetry seem to me no longer viable, visible, their flight only the flight of birds across a twilit sky, while the four horsemen ride in tanks and jets and limousines.

It will all drift away perhaps, all of my sacred lovers, like birds across the twilit sky, like the boys with whom I played such body games twenty or thirty years ago. The taste for it goes too. Age? The life of the theatre.

My culture is assaulted, and this reflection, meditation, this twilight, is its vivid proof.

Rio de Janeiro. 7-14 November 1970.

ECLIPSE

I confess: that I sometimes feel a nostalgia for Gérard de Nerval . . . and the sea . . .

JM: "Nostalgia is reactionary. The *derrière-garde* is always looking at the past and praising it. 'The good old days.' "

FLAMES

Paternalistic, patriarchal, sado-masochist, capitalist oriented: all those artists. The culture embraces me, seduction, thru the artists into my open cocksucking mind, sado-masochist oriented, and sinks downward into me and twists my balls until I let fall a frail idea
that serves the past
from which it derives

yes burn the texts
this is what the masters have finally told me
this is what the greatest of their greatness
has whispered what the failing light
hesitatingly points out
leap
we are the fire behind you
self immolation
the burning bodies of the damned
    KULCHUR
the torch
the twilight of those gods.

São Paulo, Brazil. August 1970.

CLOUDBURST:
RAIN: CLEAN SWEEP: THE WATER OF LIFE

Art begins in the artist as the expression of unfulfilled desires. Freud makes clear that unfulfilled desires are repressed sexuality. In sexuality the concrete realization of love. But the people have no time and no strength to express these desires, no way to transform into fertile experience what is heavily repressed. As civilization develops, the aristocracy pays the artist to do this. Or the Church, the spiritual master, commissions the artist. Then the bourgeoisie takes over. And all the time the artists express unfulfilled desires, and this is liberating. And impelled to do this work in order to fulfill their desires—otherwise repressed—the artists give expression to soaring concepts and ideas. They are making love when they create. And this making love discharges energy, and the aristocracy and the Church and the bourgeoisie get strong from these charges.

But now we know that the world we want is not a world in which everyone becomes a bourgeois creep, no, not a world of middle class comfort and mores. In recent times the artists have been busy reforming the bourgeoisie because that's what they were paid to do. Even the divine poets. Woe is me. But that's all over with.

Because the architects are going to stop designing houses for the bourgeois culture, and the painters are going to channel their might of color and design to stimulate millions of wide eyes instead of dilating the needle eyes of the rich and crafty. For a century we have been talking about giving this energy to the mass. We never knew how to do it. The Establishment told us we would degrade our art. They lied. It is as easy as sliding on grease to create for the discerning eye, the privileged soul. (Those days are gone because we know now how to create anti-art.) And the musicians, mathematicians, the sculptors, and song writers are going to create things which sing not of bourgeois desire but of great lusty transcendental revolutionary groan and grunt, fuck and suck. And they are already doing it with the rock and folksong art of our time— and more and more and more they come, legions, covered with petals of light, spilling the breath of life into the shacks of the damned; and the theatre like the wind will rend the oppressive heat to tatters, will break open the gates to Kiev and Jerusalem: the liberators are coming, madmen, artists: the People: who with great beauty, leaf by leaf, petal by petal, open flowering. The creation of the people which is the work of art and everything and which is what we mean when we talk about revolution.

Rio de Janeiro. 20 October 1970.

STORM WARNING:
HEAD WINDS

"Imagination as the survival kit of the brain . . ."

The imagination flies if there is no wind. Art is much wind. Head wind.

The entire condition of the slaves is deprivation. The deceptive liberal term is "underprivileged."

The slave not only gets less to eat, not only gets less culture, but the heritage of these deprivations is ultimate severity: early death: death in life already: death of the spirit: death of the spirit leads to: death of the flesh.

When artists withhold their art and energy from the struggle of the slaves, they stand with the masters, they are collaborating with those who burn food and torture the poor, and they must be overthrown.

If the imagination is not stimulated and the mind does not grow, how can the great animal figure its way out of the pit?

THE TEETH OF THE GALE
(WEST WIND)

(1) Walk right out of it. Just as Gautama walked out of the Pleasure Palace (his golden prison) into the world. Only a buddha can do that? Then we are all buddhas. (2) Bourgeois Culture is our Palace of Oppression. Jail break. (3) Art as action.

São Paulo, Brazil. 3 January 1971.

51

"1968 was the Death of a Culture. The death is not outside us. It is inside each one of us. It died right here." Georges Lapassade, tapping his breast.

Rio de Janeiro. September 1970.

52

Meditation I. 1970.

The process: one foot in front of the other, relentlessly, clinging to the ice, slipping, climbing back up, because there is nothing else to do. If we found means to stop dying, would we have to invent death to prevent the planet from becoming densely and fatally populous? We would find a way to make it work.

Death is corruption and is not intrinsic to life ... We are beyond Nature: this is the impetus of our time. Gutkind.

Je ne m'intéresse plus au théatre. Je ne m'intéresse qu'à la *politique.* Genet. São Paulo. August 1970.

I remind myself to breathe forty times a day. I coax the veins and arteries. I am confused, baffled, filled with despair, most of the time, everyday, I am hope.

There is a certain point at which meditation makes me aware of my feet folded beneath me and of the shoemaker who has trailed me since I got my first pair, his hammering driving me on all the time, he makes my feet walk over the bare ground. He carries me forward. I pay him 75¢.

We are all going forward, like a great glacier, the movement irreversible. The problem is to prevent us from destroying ourselves: accident, disaster, collision with infinite death night. We are the glacier, on it, and in it, we are history, it is not outside us, we make it bleed to death, while the boat sails we are sinking. The revolutionist rises up, out of the ice cave, builds fires on the ice, sleds; when the people rise up, uprising, the ice cracks, the glacial structure melts, but the people are above it, high.

What we are today we shall not be tomorrow.

"We are beyond nature!" Our glory!

It is necessary to find out what can be done.

Then we figure out how to do it.

And then to do it. The process.

São Paulo, Brazil. 24 August 1970.

53

Looking for our lost tribalism: create a new tribalism: the collective in which the individual is not sacrificed to the collective nor the collective to the individual. The Absolute Collective.

Essaouira, Morocco. 24 July 1969.

54

The tribe has its own charisma. The tribe is a group of people bound together by love. Therefore they find ways to survive, and therefore the tribe has a special fascination in a more or less loveless society.

Society reluctantly tolerates the gypsies because it entrusts them with preserving some of the secrets, some of the black arts. Society tolerates the experimental communes as long as it thinks that they are only working on finding solutions to the problem put before us by impractical utopian proposals. If they do not find the solutions they will wither away by themselves. If they find the solutions society will try to co-opt them or kill them off. This is the sinister secret in the armory of society's brain. The death thing.

Unlike the tribe, which expands when it is healthy, the clan is closed, bounded by blood, hierarchy, and self imposed laws. The word Tribe is being used nowadays to describe those groups which are close to those ethnic groups which never lost their relationship to the earth the sun the moon to wind water fire flesh. The primal things. Whose being is testament to some kind of natural, that is, non-artificial, tenderness for unspoiled life, life in harmony with the nature of things, and yet beyond the conflicts common to nature. The tribe is a way of grooving together. Each member is looking out for the benefit and well-being of all the members. They constitute a community in which the individuals are not alienated from each other. Moving thru a society dying of loneliness and its terrible effects (plastic love, early death, death by rivalry and enmity, death by money, by machine and murder, death by survival of the fittest, death by poison industrial gas, death by tobacco, death by aluminum oxide), the tribe, like the animals described by Kropotkin who have survived the opposing forces of the ages thru mutual aid, touches all it contacts with mysterious force and melody; it is the living symbol of useful behavior, of key, eternal rhythm. The tribe passes by; and the cold and frightened spectator, perishing in his aloneness, sees the gypsies, sees the Jews, sees the caravan of actresses and actors, scorns them for their inbred secretions, envies their ability to make it, hates, and hopes that they will transcend his hate, and knows they will.

It was only in 1964 that finally my life, The Living Theatre, began the realization of its tribal nature; and when in January, 1970, we divided, it was not to perish, but to go thru a self-imposed ordeal, in order to rebuild our tribal reality with a more intense conscious effort, in order to outwit the forces which seek to smash all tribes forever. Because the modern state cannot tolerate any group which has any feeling stronger than dependence on its own alienated/alienating dangerous doom-laden self. The tribe fights for its life in such an environment. We are fighting. When the people (from behind their windows) see us as we amble down the street they know who we are, they recognize the archetypal stride, they know we are the enemy of their state, they know we are the secret lovers of their bodies who visit them at night, we are the incubi of their unconscious, we are the meat of their dreams, we are the lickers of their spirit, we wrestle with their immaterial form, they know their state is Strong and Big and Brittle, and they know the tribe is weak and small and unbreakable.

If it is bound together by love.

This book, as record of my life, as my life itself, is a record of the struggle to become a part of a commune. The Living Theatre is that struggle. My one unique life.

The Living Theatre can't ever be a community inside a capitalistic society. It is an illusion to imagine that it can. As long as capitalism is around us, seeping into us, we have no chance. All we can do is work within the limitations until the walls fall. The walls fall. Make the music which makes them fall. The influence of the rotting structure is strong and we are weak. In this battle the weak win, because the strong are rigid and rotting. But the weak are supple and alive.

Rio de Janeiro. October 1970.

55

When authentic ritual begins, when the Gnaouas come to the courtyard and play and dance and trance out, you are drawn in, you open the windows, out on your balconies, you open yourself, because you know that what is happening is not just abstract music, you know that it is the exorcism of demons from the house, and of the entrance of good fortune, the spirit of joy. When the wine is lifted and the Hebrew words are pronounced, Blessing, you are reminded and you remind your whole self of the physical/chemical/biological/metaphysical miracle/ life: it abolishes mute and blind experience: it sanctifies being: it makes it easier to create and harder to kill.

The process of performing ritual by mechanical repetition is simply counter-revolution at work. Out of weariness: because the work we do to get thru daily life within this system does not leave us a residue of sufficient energy with which to pay attention. The problem is not centered in the nature of ritual but in the life which contains it. At the same time the ritual must relate to life in such a way that it serves to invigorate that life. Ritual cannot be institutionalized. Institutions sit on top of life, crushing it.

The warning here to the creator of ritual forms of theatre: true ritual enlivens; false ritual deadens: the techniques are empty if the action does not fill the body with its significance. This does not mean that the meaning cannot be shrouded, fertilely, in mystery which only the un-conscious can adequately comprehend.

ritual

to heighten communication   to find ecstasy   to invoke the
holy spirit   to prepare us for revolutionary action   to
open the mind   to enliven the body   to decrease fear   to
exorcise demons   to increase trust   to dispel hesitation
to transform evil   to free the heart   to arouse sexual
energy   to soften hardness   to release dreams   to free all
prisoners   to untie hands   to diminish death's dominion
a ritual to drive the old culture out of the head   to unify
the forces   to raise hope

"Ritual is something that has the body as its objective. The body is no wise a corpse in which the soul is imprisoned. Without the body the soul would be nothing but a ghost lacking the final and inescapable seriousness, the deadly earnestness of yea and nay. The body is the passive element in us, the peaceful soil in which our being is rooted. It is that which is taken as a matter of course, the constitution allotted to us by fate. It lives in the present, free from the tension of alien relation-ships, straightforward, sure of itself, sure of its own instincts; its mis-takes are called illnesses. In the body all the experiences of our fathers

106

are stored up, silent and unconscious. And not only the experience of our forebears but memories of vanished epochs in the earth's history, of life at the animal and vegetal level, nay of the starry depths themselves—all these are mysteriously lodged in the body, silent but strong ... The soul is its freedom ... In ritual we do not think with the cortex, but with the heart. Or rather, we become the vehicle of thought ... In ritual everything lives only in the present, all body." Gutkind, *The Absolute Collective.*

If the mind is corrupt, it will infect the body. JM.

Revolution as ritual acts: purification: unification: the creation of the body of the people: enlightenment, end of divisive murder. Rituals of liberation: end of nationalism which binds people to possession and to hate:

"Nationalism must needs oppress man. There can be no peace between nations, for biology knows only of war, growth, ruthless expansion. Yet there can and must be an end to all nations. The people want to free themselves of their demoniacal element and establish all ethnic qualities as but features of the Absolute Collective. All cthonic ties are relative, and everything national and racial is demoniacal substance ... The world that has turned away from idolatry and is free of possession no longer knows fear of death ... In the People, God, man and world are brought together in indissoluble unity. All creatures are contained in it from the stars to the human race, from the forces of nature to the words of human speech." Gutkind, *op. cit.*

Ritual sacrifice, ritual murder, rituals with death as object: these are the sinister products of death oriented death-dominated cultures. War is such a ritual. Capital (gold, money, as a means of exchange and as symbol of possession) is such a ritual. The State and the class system, which are hierarchical, and which wield power of life and death over and against the body of the people, are such rituals. The revolution which creates the People: a ritual act to overthrow the reign of death.

The ritual form is a discipline, an efficient form, a repeated action, a way to get things done.

56

23 Janeiro 1971. São Paulo, Brazil.

Centro Espiritista de Pai Jeronimo, Rua Mucury 107. (Bairro Jaba-quara):

A *candomblé* ceremony in the outskirts of São Paulo, the *terreiro* is located among unpaved roads in a working class district. The people are working class people, and they have lavished care and money on their small temple. The altar is bounded, on the right side and on the left, by two large plaster statues each about four feet high, one representing an "Old Black" slave, the other a *Caboclo* Indian. The congregation consists largely of their descendants. The *Caboclo* wears a large feather headdress like the North American Plains Indians wore.

The Old Black is weighted with necklaces, the kind that are worn popularly in black-dominated Bahia. White gladioli (dyed yellow and blue) and roses (in their own color) are everywhere. The back of the altar is covered with crumpled gold paper. The statues of the saints and of God the Father are larger here than in poorer *terreiros*, but the size of the two ancestors and the dominant position they occupy declare the cultural conflict.

For this ceremony tonight there are about thirty five mediums, twenty five of whom are women, mostly older than thirty. They wear elaborate Baiana costumes.

I now understand the crepe paper streamers that cover the ceilings of all the *terreiros:* Here the crepe paper is not blue like the sky as it so often is, but white and green. They are leaves. Green leaves are scattered on the floor. We are not just "out of doors," we are as if under a large tree. The mediums circle and chant. They dance; sometimes as they circle they bend as if gathering crops, sometimes they seem to be hoeing, using the machete or digging soil, sometimes they reach right and left gathering air, but all the time they dance. Drums are the only accompaniment, and they do not stop. Not until someone is possessed. One by one tonight they are possessed. The shaman, arrogant and kingly, seated on a white throne, controls his court. He picks who will next be possessed. Possession comes: then the dance stops, and everyone sits in a circle, the wide skirts making a magic ring of color inside which the possessed dances. She is possessed by the god. The god is in her body. The god manifests himself in the community. The god dances. THE GOD DANCE. Theatre which is the dancing place of the gods.

This particular occasion is the festival of São Sebastião. He is coming. His spirit (surely) will enter the community. And will dance.

57

Religious theatre. The essential flaw in all popular ritual tho it may contain the truth and the glory: it dissipates the energy, serves to content the people. The increment of apathy, the opium of the people.

The essential question then is: How do we wed the ritual so firmly with reality so that it cannot be subverted and recuperated and made to serve that which it is created to destroy?

The answer: dissociation of ritual from coercion. Law, the principles by which we codify our moral being, cannot be enforced, only studied, understood, felt, or broken. Ritual perishes if it becomes rigid. Perishes and kills. Rigidity is death.

58

Fascist theatre. When we played the *Mysteries* in Berlin in 1965, the German audience cried out:

"You are using the same techniques that the Nazis used! the same mass hypnosis! the same appeal to emotional response and that's dangerous! You have to be rational! When Julian Beck sits in the middle of a stage, lit by a spotlight directly over his head and hypnotizes us with magnetic voice and you enchain us by repeating slogans until we echo them and seduce us to come onto the stage and open our throats in a surge of ecstasy, when you make us crazy with your wordless physical contortions, with shrieking and anguish, until we want to scream, you rob us of our rational ability to see the world, to assess it and act accordingly. You make us into brainless animals. We don't want to feel, we want to think.

"The ritual form destroys the ability to rationalize, the ritual form creates masses, it destroys the individual, it sweeps him away, he loses control, he follows, and then everything is lost, the mass becomes the subject of Fascism, and Fascism uses these rituals to enslave the masses." This is what they said.

What is the difference between techniques used in *Mysteries* and Third Reich ceremonies?

Now, rituals have their own magic which is contained in their appeal to the psyche. The psyche hates and the psyche loves. And are we more prone to one than to the other? Ritual arouses feeling, and killing comes out of feeling that is non-feeling, and the new world will come out of feeling.

Ritual that is nationalistic—which extends feeling and then limits it—ritual which turns inward and not outward is toxic, murderous. In *Mysteries* we form a circle and invite the public to join us without making it a law . . . We appeal to free will . . . We arouse it.

59

Sexual Theatre.

Ceremonies of possession. *Kimbanda*. The forbidden ritual begins at midnight. It is the cry of the people for the spirit of revolution. It is the invocation of the dark anti-oppression forces, it is the ceremony in which the people summon Satan, leader of the revolt in the heaven of

ulian Beck, Avignon, 1968

2

3

2. *Paradise Now,* Brooklyn, 1968. Photo Ken Mc Laren
3. *Antigone,* Paris, November 1967. Photo Horace

4. Julian Beck, Berlin,
July 1965.
Photo Herbert Tobias

THÉATRE
AUX ouvriers

POINT nº7 de la DÉCLARATION
du LIVING-THEATRE

"Nous quittons le festival parce que le temps est venu pour nous de commencer enfin à refuser de servir ceux qui veulent que la connaissance et le pouvoir de l'art appartiennent seulement à ceux qui peuvent payer; ceux-là mêmes qui souhaitent maintenir le peuple dans l'obscurité, qui travaillent pour que le pouvoir reste aux élites, qui souhaitent contrôler la vie de l'artiste et celle des autres hommes.»

POUR NOUS AUSSI
LA LUTTE CONTINUE

6. Point 7, the Avignon Declaration

Julian Beck, meeting
discuss the occupation
the Odéon Theatre,
ris, May 1968

7

7. *The Brig,* Munich, 1965.
Photo Branko Senjor

8. Julian Beck and Judith Malina in
*The Seven Meditations on Political
Sado-masochism,* 1973

9. The Living Theatre in Brazil,
*Christmas Cake for The Hot Hole
and The Cold Hole,* São Paulo,
December 1970

8

9

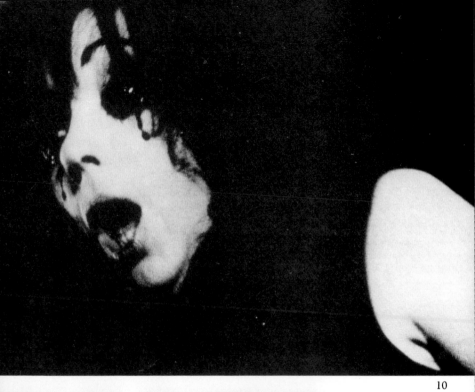

10

10. Judith Malina
in *Antigone*,
Paris,
December 1967

11. Julian Beck
in *The Maids*,
Berlin, 1966

12. Julian Beck in *The
Seven Meditations on
Political
Sado-masochism*,
Milan, 1976

12

13

13. Julian Beck in *Paradise Now*,
Geneva, August 1968

14. *Six Public Acts*,
Piazza San Marco,
Venice, October 1975

14

15. Julian Beck and Judith Malina in *The Strike
Support Oratorio*, New York City, May 1974

16. *The Money Tower*,
Pittsburgh, September 1975

17. Julian Beck in performance with the
patients at the psychiatric hospital at
Frullonne, Naples, December 1976

8. Julian Beck does the "Lion Breath,"
ysteries, Amsterdam, December 1968

19. Julian Beck and Judith Malina in
*Christmas Cake for The Hot Hole and The
Cold Hole*, Brazil, 1970. Photo Luke
Theodore

20

21

20. Julian Beck. Grand Theatre, Geneva, January 1968
21. Julian Beck and Judith Malina in prison at Belo Horizonte, Brazil, July 1971

the ruling class. It comes out of a recognition of evil rampant and out of a decision to win over the power of this evil to help free the people from eternal misery, invocation to the evil genius of Beelzebub to re-order the world, it is the playing out of a liberated anti-morality, a morality in search of a more sustaining reality than the one which prevails and which has us all in thrall. It has its magic and it is called black. It is the other side of the *Macumba* coin. *Macumba*: "I am writing about something that can't be written about." Georges Lapassade.—The *Macumba* has two sides: (1) the *Umbanda*: ritual of purification, all in white, in which the spirits of African deities, Xango or Ogum, of the revered Indians (*Caboclos*), or of the Old Black slaves (*Pretos Velhos*), or of Oriente (Prophet of the East, Muhammed), enter the body and bring to the possessed the wisdom that solves daily cares, that cures illness: the *Umbanda* is a ceremony of light; and (2) the *Kimbanda*: ritual which penetrates deep in the dark well of the earth, the mind, in the sexual organs, it is the formula for escape, conquest. Revolt. Black and Magic and White.

It is the ceremony of repressed people. It is the plan of their revolution. It is the truthful expression of a popular dream: it is desperate theatre full of hope.

The ceremony, with drums, dance, and chant, leads to possession by Satan (Exú). When he enters a medium, his falange of light does not strike the medium on the head or the back (as in the *Umbanda*), but in the pelvis, the genital region, the possession is sexual. The possessed shakes in violent physical convulsion. The women fall to their knees, face the open door, and bend backwards till their heads touch the ground behind them, spread their thighs wide, moan, groan, shriek, tremble, throb, rattle, rotate, with the red and black Emperor of Hell. Eyelids drooping, sultry, hips rolling, they rise, they are Pomba-Gira, the Devil's Mistress, his woman, and they are possessed of knowledge of evil, and they can advise you, if you are seeking advice: how to eliminate a rival, how to steal, to control, to dominate, to kill. How to do all the things that the capitalist master does or the police, all those things that the masters pretend to abhor. Exú is red. His colors are black and red. Sometimes Exú is black and depicted black in the plaster statuary, idolatry, popular in Brazil. His companion is Tranca-rua, armed with pitchfork and blade. This red and black statuette, along with the sexy whore Pomba-Gira and Exú himself occupy shrines outside the *terreiro* where the ceremony takes place. Black and red candles burn to their glory.

Possession by Black Power. The Black Sexual Power. The Dark Power of Evil. Sexual Evil. "Because there is evil in the world." These Brazilian people, fucked by the devil without getting anything in return other than servitude, give themselves over to the "evil" in order to possess it, in order to control, though they are in fact controlled. The ceremony is ecstatic. In this sexual/spiritual act comes a kind of exaltation: "Exú is Liberty," cried the shaman one night. Open sexuality is liberty. It does free. The uninhibited man is the man who will survive.

Rio de Janeiro. 17 October 1970.

60

Youth and age merge in the People. The curious device of Greek theatre which made its choruses into segments of the population: chorus of elders, chorus of women, chorus of Archons. It is the homogeneity which gives the people their reliability. I lean towards this like a plant to the light: that in the variety contained in the solidity of the mass is the ultimate viability, the victory.

An important theatrical service would be to get the crowd to recall the impulses of its youth, of its childhood, of its infancy, the impulses that grope towards paradise, the adolescent impulses towards a sexual brotherhood, or sublime love, people meeting only to create love, bodies of love like bodies of water, lakes, oceans, waves of it, out of which life, new, can again crawl out onto the beach.

Ouro Preto, Brazil. 11 March 1971.

61

the sluice of flesh in flesh:
reward for a partial life.

Carl Einhorn

El que no comprende el amor no sabe nada sobre el pueblo.

Oswaldo de la Vega

62

Popular Theatre.

One.

I did not expect to meet so much geniality among the people who perform ceremonies of possession in Morocco and Brazil. I was swept by rays of fear, the propaganda of the white culture invaded me, I was approaching this theatre with the same phony seriousness with which I enter the New York synagogue or church. But those are the institutionalized rituals of tight lipped people with rigid spines, and fear is in everything. In the *Macumba*, or in the Gnaoua sessions, where strange things happen, there is no fear. The people enter these rituals with joy. The *Djem-alf'na* in Marrakech is a tempest of joy. Rituals born of people who live in sorrow. In New York, where life is constantly being superficialized, we are sombre in our religious rites. The revolutionary culture reverses this.

The participants in these ceremonies in Morocco and Brazil seem to be largely the marginals, the ragged poor, the working classes, and in these rites they transcend their daily impotence, and experience the power of mysterious things—without the possession of "scholarly wisdom": communication with the unknown, communication with the dead, with the Devil if necessary, communication with the spirits which dispense courage and strength to survive, to hold onto hard life a little longer.

To change the sound of the music in the street, to sing, dance, chant until we are possessed by sufficient power (energy) in confrontation with daily life to change it.

The *Djem-alf'na:* everyday at 6:00 in the evening in Marrakech existence changes its colors, boredom lifts, the people flash out on what it could be like to live differently. There in that hungry country the spirit of the people nourishes itself in visionary theatre, theatre of trance: the work is to realize the visions.

Sobriety: the device of the established powers to hoodwink the masses and itself. The solemnity of the Church, Egyptian architecture: the pride of the privileged, in its heavy literature, its philosophy. As if the face of God were only revealed in abstract thought. Alienated from life, they respond only to dead mannerisms, contemplation, inactive meditation, the brahmin and buddhist aristocracy caught by the same disease. Because as soon as the asshole tightens up, and the head goes haughty and the heart cold, joy shrinks, life goes rigid, ouch.

The theatre of the revolution is the theatre of joy.

Two.

The official *carnaval* of Rio is a debauched spectacle. It has been perverted by the State, the Ministry of Tourism, and by the intangible forces of national psychoses into being the trash which color photos of it reveal. What is inspiring about it is all the stuff that gathers at its foundation. Because it is the ritual, the art, the dream of the poor realized in splendor.

This phenomenon is not remarkable. The state has been perverting the impulses of the people ever since it took it upon itself to serve wealth and to control the class struggle.

The music of the samba is African in origin, it is percussion only, and the *batrías* are composed of twenty to fifty players or more who beat an elaborate development of a 2/4 rhythm which conquers the atmosphere and changes the air current. It shuts out everything else. It changes the pulsing of the blood, and the movement of the muscles. It is accompanied by a song, a voice floating over the drums, with simple lyrics, genuine poetry.

The dance is impelled by the rhythm. It is confined to the lower regions of the body: the feet and the pelvis, but the power generated there pumps the blood, now coursing in a rhythm that is unfamiliar to the thinking head, up to the brain, in the muscles of the face. Thrill becomes available. The samba is danced alone, but it is also danced collectively, everyone is dancing, giving energy and inspiration to each other. Lines form, snakes, formulations of elaborate design, the whole people is dancing together, joy, the surest sign of the presence of God. Leon Bloy.

The poor people, the *favelados* who dwell in the slums took this form and developed it along highly theatrical lines. The lyrics became the theme for an ambulatory pageant with an elaborate and precise form. The form was invented and developed by the blacks in the nineteenth century. The blacks in their communities worked in collective creation to realize their dreams: formed guilds called *blocos* where they prepared and worked for months before the *carnavals,* contributed their own money for the upkeep of the guild and for the costumes, which they sewed themselves. Each year they invented the theme of their pageant. They made up the words, the music, the floats, the style, the choreography, the whole *mise-en-scène,* and they were the actors. Everything themselves, they worked without chiefs.

And then when the time came they poured out of their hovels, dressed in finery, and paraded thru the city transforming it for a few days into a field, elysian, of ecstasy and exhilaration.

Then they returned to their year long ritual of prolonged, mute, suffering.

The Brazilian samba guilds were authentic examples of autogestion.

But now the whole thing has become a perversion and what was beautiful and true has become ugly and false.

An organ of repression.

Perhaps the seed of that was here from the beginning, automatically, in the atmosphere of a whole society built on a master-slave pattern. Because the whole aspect of make-believe dress-up directed itself towards the imitation, by the poor, of the characteristics of the masters.

White wigs and French court gowns of satin. The love become Holly-wood, the heroism chauvinistic. They were enacting a dream of a slave, simple dream of glory, of vengeful transformation.

The state then blew it up with its foul air, business men began to contribute to the guilds, naturally then exercising control over the themes and the execution. And then the state, under Vargas, passed a law, once the whole thing became institutionalized, making it manda-tory that all the themes be patriotic. And the dreams of glory became dreams of an even more perverse content. Then came the professionals, the costumers, composers, choreographers, brought by the guilds to make the pageants more and more *Folies Bergère* and less and less the animated aspiration of the people.

Nowadays the corteges are the grotesque doubles for the funeral march. The interment of the people. In the *carnaval* they dissipate their strength and their dreams.

But I see that the strength is still there; and the dreams, unperverted, must be recumbent in the spirit.

Use this information.

I see you, Pope Clement VII, you old dog, and your whole court, right down to Medici—President Emilio Garrastazu Medici of Brazil 1969-19——always using bread and circuses to placate the children of God.

They are not placated.

Ouro Preto, Brazil. 10 May 1971.

63

"We have our I, that's real, and the Thou, that's real. And our basic condition of love, the origin of it all. Then comes everything else to interfere and pervert: economics, social systems, false values. The object is to get back to the origins. Therefore the importance of ritual: because its distinguishing feature is its profound concern with origins and our original nature." JM.

The object of ritual: the body, the origin of it all, love: love's body: the people.

64

questions. 1969.

What was the value of playing *Paradise Now* for the middle class? "So that when the revolutionists go out into the street, they—the middle class—don't call the police right away." Mel Clay.

how do we make the revolution how do we make it work how do we feed all the people how do we stop all the killing how do we make it paradise now

Playing the Play—*Paradise Now*—brings the performer face to face with these questions *in between* performances: questions are the performer's preparation for playing *Paradise Now*.

Ethics. But why didn't Pascal or Kant discuss the nature of the ethical position within the capitalist authoritarian scheme? Because they did not yet know what the social movements of the nineteenth century were going to reveal. Time as dimension; one sees as far as time, one's time, permits.

We have reached that point in our development—civilization has brought us here—at which the questions are the whole thing of it. Nothing else is interesting. No matter what you do the other questions are always there. Questions: the beginning of answers.

The theatre is frightening because it deals with the mysteries and the mysterious questions. For centuries the theatre asked: who are we where have we come from where are we going

Now it asks: what is it where is it going what can be done what am i doing with my one unique life at this moment when the collective genius of humankind must answer the question: how can our planet survive?

Torino, Italy. 19 October 1969.

65

Workbook entries.

Antigone: Berlin: 27 August 1966:
At the age of forty one i doubt that i have the courage, the ability to take the *Antigone* trip. To drive that far without knowing how much gas is in the tank.

Antigone: Kiel: 5 March 1967:
now that the *Antigone* trip has been made
i see the doubt I felt at the start
was the void
not into which i had stepped
but which was inside me:

i was emptying myself
in order to make it new

Paradise Now: Napoli: 24 May 1967:
The first stare at it:
Again it's the void. I see nothing. I get no reading. Only the determination to go somewhere else than where I am.

Everything else that I consciously know is wrong. The problem with logicians is that they leave out what they don't know consciously and express only what they consciously know. That is why they always sound wrong.

Because I cannot push the revolution fast enough with logic, I push
towards what I cannot consciously control, let the wind blow thru, let
the revolution come. Let go of the panel board.

Paradise Now: Paris: 17 December 1967:
to envelope the audience in such
joy that the impossible seems
possible

Paradise Now: New York City: December 1968:
The original intention:
"to envelope the audience in such
joy that the impossible seems
possible"

therefore
paradise now became the creation of
a dialectic for action
that could bring about the beautiful nonviolent anarchist
            revolution

what else
could produce
"such joy"?

66

we did *antigone* in 1967
        so that:
        antigone's example
        after 2,500 years of failure
        might at last move
        an intellectual paying audience
        to take action
        before it is
too late.

("For she who saw it all could only help the enemy." brecht, accusing
antigone of waking up "too late."

and we:
        too late:
                believing that out of *style*
        could come:
                political satori.

paul goodman:
"the athenians, after a performance of *the trojan women*
are sadder and wiser."
BUT THEY CONTINUE PLUNGING ALONG!
        INTO PERFIDY! WAR AND SLAVERY!
"by confronting us
with a more meaningful universe,
it (*the trojan women*) leaves us with a saner
                whole philosophy
                (more congenial to pacifism
                in so far as pacifism
                is the truth)." p.g.

                BUT WE CONTINUE PLUNGING ALONG!

                        and all this has to do with why
                        art and beauty
                        are not enough

                                        Look there! there! in the water!
                                rising up!
the foam! spraying!
        beyond art:
                the act of defiance
                like antigone —
the act! which will bring down the structure!
        and not
                too late.
                        don't bother with boats,
                        don't bother with the theatre.

uprising

67

Letter to a wound.

An art which does not address itself to the horrendous problem of the division of the world into classes increases the universal anguish.

Until the money system is over, the classes exist.

First we do the difficult, then we do the impossible. (Piscator, citing the old adage.)

First we get out from under the yoke of the economic system.

Raise consciousness to understand this and feel it sufficiently to act. Stop all other activity. Everything else as waste. Hurry.

Brussels.   14 December 1969.

68

Verge of the new work. Brussels. 17 December 1969.

What was the past all about?

> The collective creation.
> Concept of a theatre company, a working group, as
>   anarchist commune.
> Free theatre. And with it improvisation: creation on
>   the spot.
> Itinerant theatre company as programming unit, a way
>   of living on the edge, outside of the tight center.
> Counter-violent theatre. Theatre as spokesman for anarchy,
>   for nonviolent revolution, for revolution.

Why am I down tonight?
Spleen?
Sugarlack?
The skin under my eye like a turtle's, like dry leaves?
The burning forest?
The insignificance of boats?
The tightness in my balls?
The fading of time, of hope, of people?
The fading, as everything whitens out?

Questions. 1969.

Because you are what you eat
and you work with what you have.

Libido Blues, Ego Blues, this is what I have: Bourgeois Blues: we must
not let them win and stop the work as they would wish:
danger:
because we will have these conditions: Bourgeois Blues:
until we change the system which produces them
and the food it gives us and doesn't give us to eat.

69

The Living Theatre functions, says Judith, so that the idea of what it is
exists differently in each individual member's head. Then we each let
each other do whatever each of us wants to do to develop that vision.
To this degree it is what I want it to be and what Roy Harris or Carl
Einhorn wants it to be. And if we fall out of love with that vision,
whether it is succeeding or failing to develop, we go away. I give it
everything. I imagine everyone in it does. If this is so then I am no more
authoritarian nor authority than anyone else.

In the community there are always problems, conflicts, and sickness.
The community is unified (woven together) by love, finding persistent
expression in warm affection and physical contact. We always worked
with sexual hangups, and hacked away at refining them. We are more a

symbol of sexual liberty than the living examples of it. But the force of our aspiration carries the message.

The center is the work. So long as the work gets done. Other things are secondary to it. That's where the sovereignty is. With the exception, which makes it free, that the work can be sacrificed at any time when another need takes priority: madness, jealousy, illness, conflict: provided the group survives. Or until it needs to dissolve or transform itself.

Long ago Judith put the question: How could there be a law without coercion? To have laws which are principles which can be freely broken whenever anyone feels the need to do so without shattering the sense of the order of things.

This would be possible in a communal situation, given the changes in character and behavior which we can expect within an anarchist-communist culture.

70

Meditations on Theatre I.

people go to the theatre for the light of omar where else will they find it people go to the theatre to see the dragon outwitted people go to the theatre to blend with the wind people go to the theatre for the keys to salvation people go to the theatre to learn how to breathe people go to the theatre for sexual liberation spiritual liberation for manifestos people go to the theatre for no base motive

The theatre that we are annihilating
is the theatre which,
instead of liberating,
gave allegiance to class culture, alienation,
insufficient food

Avignon to Lyon, France. 16 May 1970.

we are a movement
the critics try to divide us
and play us against each other
stop us from being a movement
but we are a movement

São Paulo, Brazil. 23 January 1971.

After all your whole life is a play. Now we come to the question: what kind?

The struggle to break the form is paramount. Because we are otherwise contained in forms that deny us the possibility of realizing a form (a technique) to escape the fire in which we are being consumed.

Rio de Janeiro. 14 October 1970.

The Polish Theatre Laboratory Company and The Living Theatre spent a night together talking on the roof of a small hotel near the Piazza di Spagna in Rome, July 1967.

We discussed our respective methods: how Grotowski's is authoritarian and separates the individuals, and how ours tries to be communal.

Compensation, says Grotowski, indicating the political systems in which both groups respectively live. He immediately psychoanalyzes, and pins it, in his style.

Things are simpler and far more complicated.   Genet.

In order to create mass mentality, the cult of the individual must be destroyed. Mao.

The aware individual creates a lively mass, by stimulating dialogue between the cells.

The mass that crushes the individual makes dead flesh.

The individualist culture that fragments us—cuts us up into little pieces—is committing suicide.

Ouro Preto, Brazil. 29 November 1970.

all primitive theatre
        (theatre in its origins) rites
        of and close to the people,
speaks in symbols,
        parables;
the theatre of realism is the invention of the Duke of
        Saxe-Meiningen
        a Duke
made for the aristocracy by the
        aristocracy;
realism is the language of the
        aristocracy
        because aristocrats are so far from life.

Compensation.

Rio de Janeiro. 23 October 1970.

71

Repressive architecture is rampant. "Frozen music." Cold, yes. And the "music," surely the music that thrilled the court. The priests. The emperor. The pretentious merchants. The Board of Directors. The Parthenon? Its geometry? Its splendor? Beauty and philosophy are not enough.

Who lugged the stones? (Brecht). Who smelted the bronze for Van der Rohe's whiskey building?

When I was seventeen modern architecture filled us with pride: at last, we believed, the principles of art were regaining dominion in architecture after a century of dominion by the taste of the philistines.

Architecture would no longer be sacrificed on the altar of commerce. How conditioned we were!

There is basically no difference between Van der Rohe's whiskey building and Versailles. Nor between Frank Lloyd Wright's dwellings for millionaires and the domineering chateaux and castles that rule the European landscapes. The taste that we admire (?) is the taste of the Rulers of Slaves, that was the taste that Wright and Van der Rohe were catering to.

Naturally Wright and Van der Rohe ended up designing courthouses and jails.

Buckminster Fuller builds for the Army. Watch out.

The Chicago Conspiracy trial (1970) took place among thousands of other trials upholding the corroded majesty of the law in a majestic building, a factory producing prison terms, Van der Rohe's palace of oppression. The form of the building is rigid, relentless. The oppressors admire this: the cold formality, reflecting its cruel function.

Judge Julius Hoffman to William Kunstler, defense counsel for the Chicago Seven: "Mr. Kunstler, there is a great architect, Mies Van der Rohe, who lately left us. He designed that lectern as well as the building, and it was a lectern and not a leaning post. I have asked you to stand behind it when you question the witness."

Pomposity, inflexible, rampant, the tall straight rigid buildings, with the straight proud men, the ramrod spines, not bent by labor, the polite voices, everything designed to cut the heart out. Architecture shapes and is shaped by the culture.

The theatres reflect the same culture, sterility, pomp, and judgment. Burn the theatres. Give us an architecture with human values.

The Seven Lamps of Architecture:

The light of human values.

The oil that ends life isolated, compartmentalized, alienated from one another in our houses.

The lamp that refuses to burn for money. But the architects are working for money, they have lost their humanity, stones.

The lamp that does not burn for the ruling class: no more homes for capitalists, ministers.

The lamp of the poor: only the best efforts for the poor, the sharing of light.

The lamp of the invention of revolution which will be lit by the question: "But who will pay us if we build for the poor? Who will pay for the materials?"

The lamp that lights the building for the divine taste of slaves, building theatres for them, places where they can gather to exorcise demons and celebrate the glories, and extend mind and senses, and create the body of love . . .

As for me, I don't want to work in those repressive courtroom shaped theatres anymore.

I am speaking even of the theatres at Delphi and Syracuse, Taormina and Epidaurus, where the splendor and pleasure of watching blinds the eye of truth.

Croissy-sur-Seine, France. 18 April 1970.

72

The bourgeois instinct recoils from the terminology of the socially conscious artist.

The bourgeoisie wince every time they hear the term THE MASSES. As if the masses were something coarse, without identity, without ego, frightening.

The bourgeoisie do not consider it tasteful to speak of proletarian literature. They want literature for themselves. They refer to moralists as sick. "Morality hurts art; art should not judge."

For the bourgeoisie the needs of art can be more important than the needs of the people.

73

The philosophy of the classical theatre was a stab in the flesh of living women and men. Over and over again. The very concept of fate, of the fanshaped hand of destiny, has held us back from doing what we ought to do. A whole five act aesthetic was promoted to make us feel more helpless in face of arbitrary riches and death.

The poets muddy the waters to hide their lack of profundity, says Zarathustra. And, I agree, poetry on the page does that; but poetry as life, yours or mine, does not, Zarathustra.

I thought you to be the great in everything, in guilt and in glory, you're but a puny, James Joyce, even you, you're but a puny with dubious theory of circular history.

Literature and its medals and libraries: part of the attempt to invent games to hide the death thing.

All the great plays used to end with dying. Praise of death. Because the dying focus on what's happening. Death in these plays is an individual trip. As soon as the plays got social (19th Century) they stopped ending with death all the time. Because during the 19th Century Industrial Revolution, the problem was no longer the problem of an individual and his/her battle with virtue and villainy. Or, with Strindberg, life was more tragic than death. With Strindberg the glory is always right at hand, the mysterious trip is immediately accessible, but we ignore that possibility by clinging to madness and our paltry ways—to the mean level on which we choose to communicate especially in our daily life. With our daily self-imposed psychological system.

Death isn't the principal subject of modern theatre, tho we are much possessed by death and labor and love under its shadow. In a society, a civilization in fact that is doing a *Totentanz*, such as we are doing now, what do you do? The theatre of social awareness (there is no awareness without social awareness) has to be more interested in how to live than in how to die.

74

Meditation II. 1970.

os homens perderam o ritmo da natureza e o poema ajuda os homens a reencontrar esse ritmo. arlindo castro.

men lose the rhythm of nature, poetry helps them find it again.

with that rhythm, judgment and action are less in danger, less in a position of being dangerous.

jazz, it bends the mind. so that you think differently. it changes the understanding of reality, it projects different images, it has nothing to do with politics, but it changes politics.

we are in a revolution. it began to bud a few hundred years ago, this lotus. jazz is one of its petals. psychoanalysis. pacifism. petals petals. trotsky. louise michel. the 18th century's struggle to create conditions that would protect freedom of press, speech, religious worship, public assembly, creed. petals. the diggers. *les phalenstéres.* nestor makhno. 10,000 petals. 10,000 elements.

but look ... it is dying ... while it's maturing ... can you wait? ... how long? ...

you either consciously elect to be an element in this struggle (a lotus is a struggle) or you are manipulated by it and subjected to its vicissitudes, its victories and defeats, slime on the floor of the sea, wreckage.

i eat, i scrounge for money, i always find it. the white bourgeois intellectual community will support me. i have that security. i struggle because my soul is discontent: i yearn for things that are not, i always hear the drowning sound of prisoners falling into jail: i hear the blast of two hundred voices inside the steel concrete glass brick cage of the tombs—the barbaric jail on white street in new york—all jails are barbaric—i hear the crashing of tin dishes, like stereo turned up too much, too much. that sound. it never leaves me, till the last jail falls, it binds me to reality, because my life has been pleasure, i have to hold on to the sound of that racket, or i would die smothered by the bounty.

i have to find artificial stimuli (spiritual impulses) to play the iconoclast, the liberator, the comrade.

when we rave we speak of seeing the face of god. the face of god is the face of the people?

at every moment i need preventive measures against decadence. that's why i have to prime the pump, with flaming rhetoric, hyperbolic poetry, to keep myself from going limp and succumbing to the pleasure garden.

that's why i keep alive the sound of the tombs, and see by my side, whenever i reach into my pocket for money, the infected eyes of the beggar boy in taxco, 1949.

because i am not black, i am not creature of third world, i am not working class, i am not lumpen, i am not oppressed female. i am middle class jewish bright aristocratic polish hungarian french german american bohemian beat surrealist vegetarian homosexual hippie yippie free and lover. poet communist anarchist revolutionist. the slings and arrows of the boys on the street, the cops, the law, are fuel for the machine of me. and my slave mentality. i fight the pain because i like the pain.

i ate well the first seven years of my life. the development of the brain largely depends on the nourishment you get in the first seven years. so the children of poverty are not only being denied the comfort of a full belly, but the glory of the minds they're born with.

the black people's stimulus is their own reality. i may glow, but they are flaming. i can add my oil, my fire to theirs but the subject matter of their theatre is far more important, here and now, than my (eternal) soul, more important than the realization of my visions of another state of being. and they know this, that's why they can, with honor, reject me, and my offers, tho we all know that soon we must mass together for the great assaults to come, the long hard pull, our long march.

talking to people i get the feeling that the people basically want the revolution, would want the beautiful nonviolent anarchist revolution but they want someone else to do it for them. this has nothing to do with laziness, but with fear and trembling before the moment.

the rite of study has to include lessons in the joy of taking action. just as in *al f'tah* the initiates must learn to bite off the heads of live chickens, *hinkemann*, degradation, the rite of study has to include lessons in the joy of taking action. passage from a passive to an active life. after which passive forms of life could be enjoyed rather than endured.

when we say we don't want to make judgments, or when the people i talk to in the street sound afraid of making choices that would draw them into action, it's that we don't want to be guilty, we don't want to be responsible, we don't want to make mistakes, and we don't want to pronounce anyone or anything guilty. basically an anarchist attitude, this hesitation. not weakmindedness because not indecision, it is a strong act of refusal to rule.

i'm never able to get all the information i need. i want to get past intuition: i am impelled to study. simon vinkenoog: "u and i we just never stop going to school." but there are other impulses: the impulse to be well equipped in this struggle, comrade, the fear of being unprepared.

a tightrope that has to be walked. apocalypse: not enough time to complete this rite of study, and that is what bobby seale means when, quoting mao, he puts it, we may be right and we may be wrong but we have to do it, seize the time.

the dead and the distant living, in their recorded and ordered literature, can't give me all the answers, no matter how many nights i use for study rather than love. there is always the point at which you have to make choices independently. as a child i was always afraid of the day when i would be on my own, which they told me was coming. the security of books, my father, of the authoritarian guide: like the bible, the talmud, marx or mao. the moment when you figure it out alone without the little red book, out of your own heart of experience, out of the soul of the cortex: entering the moment: staking everything on it: the existential flowering: being alive.

you work for the long run, the super-objective. the super-objective affects everything that is done in terms of the short run, and thereby speeds up the total revolution.

if there is only a short run aim, without long run comprehension, the best intentions easily fall into reformism and strengthen the status quo, the best intentions serve the very thing that created the bad condition and always will create the bad condition and will create new bad conditions because the existence of bad conditions is an essential for (1) the state: bad conditions are its *raison d'etre*, it must then control and order them, and (2) capitalism: it has to have slaves, therefore it manufactures misery.

the system says that jails exist because of the character of man.

the purpose of the theatre is to open the doors of all the jails.

the system seeks to reduce engagement by limiting the mind, numbing the body, outlawing the spirit, and shaming the imagination: alienation.

the theatre is a popular form of mass reunion thru which the permanent revolution can pass, picking up arms.

everything then ought to be theatre. a fleet of boats to carry us till we are strong enough to fly, to reverse the downward trend of the sky, the oppressive atmosphere. we must make our own weather. in the rhythm of life.

and still,
even as i look for it, i find myself
losing the rhythm of life, everything becomes unreal,
and will a poem help
me find it again?

look in the mirror everyday of your life and you will see death at work.
cocteau.

132

look in the eye of the sexual organs of the revolutionist and you will see life at work.

look in the eye of the sexual organs of the killer and you will see life dying to work.

look in the eye of the sexual organs of the poor and you will see god at work.

this is the book that never gets finished. because it is part of a process that is not supposed to end: the principle of permanent revolution.

São Paulo, Rio de Janeiro, Ouro Preto. 1970.

75

Twilight zone. Last look back.

Part of my immediate heritage, reading, writing, grafted onto me by my family, Jewish.

Judaism (and consequently the Jewish family) place a sacred-key-like emphasis on the mystery of writing and reading, the holy word, the connection with the divinely inspired past, the message to the ever more and ever equally divine present and future, the word, spoken, written, read, studied, amplified, was magnetic centre of my childhood, youth, and early manhood. Later I learned about action. We Jews who so strongly hold to the collective, and seek realization thru the collective, seek collective communication thru the medium of writing and reading. Seeking community thru communal study. It has to do with the conquest of death.

A nineteen year old boy, his hair beautiful and long, January 1969, says, Nobody reads anymore we have lots of books and we read *in* them but no one reads a book from start to finish anymore, we don't think that way. 1969.

The spoken word, the human face: the maxima of experience. Gutkind.

Alphabetization. Reading: Rite of Study. "He who reads too much corrupts himself." Mao, the avid reader, the mountain writer, the poet general.

Reading without action is vampirism: you take in and don't give out.

It is good to know in Wichita what is happening in Bogotá. It is good to think in Chicago what Malatesta thought in Naples. Pound's homage to the translators: he who ferries back across the Styx the dead words. Orpheus. Chorus. It is good to read what the enemy is writing so that you can use it to undo him. It is good to read the secrets of Lorca because they unlock the pit of the stomach when so much other language and action are tying things up.

Everything I read goes into my arsenal, my garden, my factory, my wheatfield, my decomposition unit.

Alphabetization. Unlocking of mysteries. Keys. The creaking hinge.

Why do modern governments which discouraged literacy fifty years ago now encourage it? Because a nation's greatest resource, the modern technocratic state has discovered, is its intelligence.

The drawing of sides.

Judith: "Yes I read anarchist literature for instance, but that is not why nor how I became an anarchist, not by reading a lot of material, more by having read a single article that fell into my hands by chance. Emile Armand's piece on Individualist Anarchism, written for the *Anarchist Encyclopedia,* and I knew right away and showed it to Julian who picked up on it right away; sometimes something that you have been feeling and thinking for a long time finds expression in a piece of writing, and then you go back into history and study and look for answers to questions that are tangled in your head, and that's one kind of reading, and nowadays, 1970, I mostly read newspapers, especially the radical underground press." *Croissy-sur-Seine, France. 13 March 1970.*

To read and thereby learn much more than what you read. Because the process of learning to read also trains the mind to do other things . . . to

134

reason ... to decode ... to put words together ... to make rapid connections ... to imagine ... to figure out ... to figure out how to make the post-scarcity society into the post-scarcity anarchist society.

The beauty of information.

Croissy-sur-Seine, France. 14 March 1970:
French television comes and asks us to talk about literature, the books in our lives, for color TV. That's how they do it. They don't read—the rich, who always (Scott Fitzgerald) think they are better than we are— they look at TV and they want to see someone sitting in their house and talking about literature, so that they, the rich, can feel cultured. You, the special person, tell them what books you read that made you so smart and famous.

They want you to talk about poetry. That would mean the abasement of Neruda, Wordsworth, Breton. We refuse. We talk about anarchism. We talk about how literature—communication—doesn't mean anything if it doesn't end in action. Always the same thing.

Blake, Brecht, Rimbaud had something to do with bringing us to the point at which we do what we are doing now: militant persistence to change the world. But Rimbaud in the context of the last one hundred years. Until a short time ago he who said *changer la vie* could influence you towards trying to do it. Rimbaud in 1970 is the pleasure of Mr. Coldness and Mrs. Moregold. Do they read him? It doesn't matter.

They count him, like they count gold and stocks and bonds and mines and real-estate. They count him among their treasures and accomplishments, they process Lorca by building a wall around him. Lorca who brought us to this point, and who can bring us no further.

We have to go beyond Rimbaud and Lorca, we have to go beyond Marx and Bakunin. Beyond Breton and Trotsky. Buber and Gutkind. Beyond Gandhi. They brought us so far. Yesterday. It doesn't work anymore. The cruelty of our time is such that to talk of the trees (Brecht) feels like a crime. Words unless they activate revolution are against our interest. To be seduced by language into private pleasures (while the blood runs out): in this sense art and literature, no matter to what degree they may extend conscious awareness, are serving the interests of the killers.

In France you can't sell *Tricontinentale*, the review documenting the

Latin American revolutionary movement(s). In France they just out-
lawed Carlos Marighella's *For the Liberation of Brazil*. In France, and in
Brazil, you can buy Rimbaud. Look to it.

76

Autodestruction:

I

Roy Harris: "The system itself is very strong and invades
everyone's life:
but in fact it isn't working: it is destroying itself:
it answers neither the needs of society nor of the people:
Nerve Gas! they are burying it in the sea! they don't know how else
          to get rid of it!
it is becoming obvious to all the people:
that to maintain the system will mean
the end of the planet.
The system is falling:
and we can help it fall faster:
by pushing."

Autodestruction: our senses of awareness are so cut off
          (alienation)
we don't see right we don't hear what's going on don't smell don't
          feel don't taste reality:
and therefore all the information we are feeding our brains
          computers
is false information.
Ergo: the product of the brain, its thought, its rationale:
is based on misinformation: lies: ergo:
the brain itself is a quasi lie machine:
the big lie.

II

Rivera knew, who painted Ford's workers and the history of the
      earth in his great murals in Detroit,
that the cars would not be better, would not be run on solar
          energy, not be uncorrupt (free of built-in obsolescence and
          commercial lust)
until the star of revolution rose.

Rivera died before the star rose and the people breathed.

III

In the Pantheon of Liberators:
Gandhi, Fourier, Godwin,
      Proudhon, Buber, Rudolf Rocker,
          with apples for the people,
          who with Liebknecht and Luxembourg
          foresaw the end of hated labor:
Chief Joseph, Winstanley, Alexander Berkman,
          with organized love,
Proudhon and Marx claw at each other
          to find the truth,
Bakunin proclaiming that there can be no leaders,
Emma Goldman, Simone Weil, Tolstoi,
Joe Hill, Frankenstein's Creature,
Thomas Merton, Eluard,
Lorca, dorsal finned
      yellow tan cock
      with black pubic hair and words
      formed in his automatic gonads,
          his fancy plums,
and the unknown:
      Richard Wei, George O'Connor, Wesley Roberts:
      the faces working at the famous Ford assembly line:
      all those faces Rivera painted in 1934:
      all those dead nameless beauties:
who expended themselves in desperation:
waiting each morning the rising of the black star:
(our black sun against a red sky)
the morning of the beautiful nonviolent anarchist revolution:
and all dead with Rivera before the star rose.

IV

Examining possibilities.

In the midst of the autodestruction:
    can the theatre of the revolution re-invigorate awareness
        so that the information fed to the brain
            is no longer false?
      so that bad bread
           (the white bleached flour commercialized
              aristocracy taste)
                  will cease to be manufactured?
Because the workers will refuse to do it, saying:
      "No more autodestruction!"
That's the point at which the system will fall. Push.
      "No more leaders!"
That's the point at which Rivera's star will rise: Push. Push.

Erie (Pennsylvania), U.S.A. 15 December 1968.

77

When the people play the role of heroic liberator, they will play the great theatre of our time.

Nothing else can be great theatre because greatness is defined by the degree to which it fulfills the needs and the potential of the time.

The performer will not be playing the liberator of her/his own puny personal problems, like Hamlet, played in hermetic environments, but on the stage of the world: the liberation.

David against Goliath: the people against the police: that's where the great theatre has been performed, and in the southern United States where little girls and old men put their black bodies in front of an oncoming mass of white flesh white brains and proclaimed the turning of humankind from darkness to light. And we have witnessed the pathetic turn of that great movement, tragic flaw of white bourgeois infection as the followers of the sweet Lutheran King asked for a share of bourgeois production and bourgeois law and bourgeois order. Up till then they beamed truths that Hamlet never dreamed of. They gleamed in their innocent blackness more than old whitehaired Lear in his corrupt and kingly misery. How corrupt the history of drama is, how it deceived us.

The theatre of the Black Panthers: eloquent, they do not pretend, like their enemy, white society, to be nonviolent. They are fighting for life and liberty and for the people. And the demonic forces that claim to be egalitarian prove themselves to be the contrary by not listening to the cry of the people. We are coming out of a period of delusion now, as we come to realize that all democracies are masks for fraud and that democracy cannot work inside a money system and that money, in fact, creates racism.

Meanwhile, while the blacks play their roles, showing the whites that the blacks are the heroes of our time, we—the anarchist-pacifist-activists—we do our work, preparing, learning our parts, training, till we go out and do our act. The issue of violence does not alienate the anarchist-pacifist struggle from the struggle of the blacks; together we are creating the play called *Revolution* (in the course of which racism, money, violence, are destined to die). The blacks, more than any other artist-prophets in our time, are showing how to play this play. Fearlessly. Above all.

78

The cry. The process. A second beginning:

It's all becoming clearer, what it's all about. They taught us so little about it. Because they all really thought it was almost something else.

How beautiful it all is, and how beautiful we all are in this terrible and beautiful film of becoming. How the experience of beauty validates the pain. Compensation? Masochism. On this planet so many errors, bound in the prisons of our societies and our ways, a man has to vault out. No one tells you how. You have to learn. How to open to collective thinking and feeling. What finally conducts you to this city? What makes us begin to plan getting out of the oubliette in which we all get thrust. What congregated might of storm and forces finally moves us? It happens to a whole generation at the same time: and we begin to struggle out.

Twenty years ago I thought it was art. I thought that the practical influence of poetry could make of poets "the unacknowledged legislators of the world." Shelley.

I thought it was a process of awakening the moral chambers of the mind, so that the imagination and spirit of man could spread out their wings and rise out of the shadow world of material greed. Bourgeois rationalization. How will I ever be sure that I am beyond the influence of the class and culture in which I was born? Ripping. Navigating. Wave after wave, the life of the theatre.

Those who are hungry cannot wait. Everytime someone dies, it is too late. And everytime a generation grows up and dies (in agony) it is too late. What event touched the nerve in my being that finally twitched at this point and sent me reeling out of the theatre and into the world? The Oedipal urge to murder my father? The blind beggar boy in Taxco? The attempt to assuage middle-class guilt? Whose cry did old Marx hear?

It is always there. It is the howling of the wretched. Everyone hears it. But the system, fanatically driven, clogs our senses.

Many hear it tonight. The process of making the sound heard.

What poetry opens the ears? What holy act or accident? Once that sound gets thru you never forget it, you never don't hear it again, it never lets you alone, you can try to kill it off, the ghost of it will haunt you. Life becomes bearable only as you seek to alleviate the pain of it. Therefore in the theatre, in life, I scream: in order to be heard, to transmit the sound, to open myself and let the truth cry out.

79

The Department of Political and Social Order, Brazil's secret police is concerned with two things, and two things only: "subversion" (revolution) and drugs. The Department of Political and Social Order (commonly referred to as Dops, abbreviation for *Departamento de Ordem Politica e Social*) is notorious for the methods it uses to obtain information from revolutionists. They have a small hand-held electric generator, made in USA, which U.S. forces in Vietnam use to attach to field telephones, and the wires that extend from it get attached to the victim's hands, feet, penis, or get wrapped tightly around the balls or breasts. Sometimes, if the victim is hanging suspended from the "parrot's perch"—a pole that gets thrust between the back of the knees and the elbows after the wrists have been tied to the ankles and the pole lifted so that it rests on two desks,—sometimes the wires get stuck into the vagina or asshole. Then "the man" turns the generator. The Dops also administer severe beatings, they break bones, they smash fingers, they stick rubber tubes into the throat and nostrils and pour water down them. Victims have drowned this way . . . It is not uninteresting that these methods for obtaining information are applied not only to revolutionists but, routinely, every day of the Brazilian week, to people picked up on marijuana charges, people picked up for holding as little as a single joint. I have stood outside the room, impotent, wiped out by my inability to do anything while the screams of the tormented potheads tore into me.

The corollary between drug consciousness and drop-out, between drug consciousness and revolt, between drug consciousness and black skin, between drug consciousness and black flag, between drug consciousness and red skin, between drug consciousness and red flag, between drug consciousness and vision, between drug consciousness and love.

They are persecuting the blacks and the Jews and the Arabs and the communists and the drug students and the school children and the workers. They are, as always, persecuting many minorities: but they are also persecuting the majority: in Brazil 50% of the population is classified as Lumpenproletariat. Persecution: to try to wipe out the gypsies: Capital vs. Woodstock Nation, Romans vs. Christians, Inquisition vs. Heretics, White Man vs. Indians, Bourgeoisie vs. Trippers (especially political trippers), the jailors vs. the liberators. PERSECUTION: spiritual/material genocide: there are millions of us whose lives are heightened thru the use of drugs. Who is the State to decide what I am to do with my head? The state is not worried about my head, but about its own. Not my state.

Problem: psychosexually the world is in the grip of the steel glove of such perversion and frustration that the death wish is being squeezed out like vaseline . . . what Freud discovered in our dark closet . . . that drawer which pulls from the pelvis out . . . and psychosexually we have developed a civilization form which is directed towards death, Doctor, madness doom. There are drugs which relieve us of the death wish, which carry life giving impulses: the imagination to see things for what they are and to project formulas for development, Doctor. We are persecuted, Doctor, because we are veering away from death, but this they are too stupid to know. By "they" I mean the ones in charge who compute everything but they don't know how to compute the life impulse.

We are going so far out that they will never be able to catch us.

Because, forced to it, we can get high on our enthusiasm. Enthusiasm to smash the state. Our ability to get high is our singular protection. It teaches us the secrets of life. These secrets are in our songs while the heavy hand of death writes all the State's laws.

"The trouble with being a genius is that you have to sit around so much of the time doing nothing." Gertrude Stein. What she was saying has to do with entering a state of self-induced trance: reveries . . . high . . . Food of Paradise.

Turning the audience on. Increasing conscious awareness. To take the head where it has not been, and the body, by changing the chemistry. To undo will power. To alter the will. To alter the body, which as we know, Doctors . . . is not doing so well.

Who says we are mistreating the body with our drugs? We are honoring it and its ability to change like the moon, like an embryo, like a poem, like a day, like a war.

Certainly we can imagine the time (after the great uprising) when, free of the oppressive conditions of our pre-revolutionary world which prevent us from getting high on love and zest, when we—without taking smoke into our lungs or chemicals into our blood—float way up, high, lifted by unfettered imagination, by our free spirits. But today the unfettered imagination, like freedom, is not part of our prison world reality. Takes mighty effort, magic drugs.

142

The theatre as vehicle for the initiation of changes, what we have called the theatre of changes: that is why the theatre must be as high as possible: it must get the audience high: theatre as ritual to free public consciousness. Great great hordes going to the theatre, Dcotor, to get high ... and free. Away from the undertow, the bring-down. High theatre in which the people are given the stimulus and the fuel to go beyond themselves. Uprising.

... the casualties ... the O.D.'s ... the bad shit ... the addictive slavery ... the hell trips ... the scars ... Jenny ... all of whom were victims of drugs because they were rebels against everything in a world of sorrow and prohibition ... freedom now ... change life ... drugs as an allure to living—not drugs as retreat, annihilation: to make life more alluring than the death-inviting drugs ... this is the strategy: not more anger, rigor, cruelty.

There are drugs which free you and drugs which enslave. Pot and hash liberate. Heroin and opium enslave. They become masters. Masters (Genet has shown us) become an addiction for slaves (and slaves for masters). The revolutionist opposes all forms of enslavement.

The establishment does not like drugs because it feels insulted that the user rejects the keys to life offered by the establishment, rejects the establishment's ways. Vengeance.

The establishment does not like drugs because the establishment is cruel. It takes pleasure in punishment. It hunts. It imprisons. It tortures. Its way of life (death) does not permit it to understand.

The establishment is never able to look further than the limits prescribed by its vision, by the feelingless state in which it exists.

The State does not like liberators of the imagination because it senses that free imagination is simply going to win in the struggle.

1968: The year they began to use helicopters and chemicals to defoliate the marijuana fields of Mexico, the year we began to get searched every time we crossed a border, the year the establishment began its war to wipe out all drugs just because they tend to free the mind of man: to wipe out plants that nourish the imagination: imagination, faith, beauty, love, truth, are forces like the atom: we are discovering their strength little by little: and faster and faster and faster: and we are going to unleash these forces: flowering ecstasy: the stalking plants:

143

The dream—the collective dream—the vision of earthly paradise inspires the revolutionary uprising. The Structure tries to obliterate this dream, substituting its own "image of the model life." Cannabis and psychedelics smash such images and stir the collective dreams.

Hypocrisy: governments that bewail death by overdose and attach electric wires and wage war.

The imagination will retaliate with secret sprays, chemical campaign, and with poetry, with the highest expression of our highest feelings and thoughts and the trite mind will grow wondrous, the police subverted . . .

It will take us 20-30-40 years, which isn't long because we are resolved: to live to do it: in our own life time, work, smoke, rise up, get high, fly, defy everything that imprisons, tortures, kills, change it, transform it: "this is our triumph" (Vanzetti), our inevitable ecstasy, I am high now, and it is clear to me: the situation in which food, love and freedom are rampant—post scarcity communist-anarchism—is simply irresistible, inevitable. The spirit of it is in the weed . . .

It is of more than just mystic significance that the United States government burns both wheat and marijuana . . .

Ferrara, Italy. May 1966.
Detention Cells, Department of Political and Social Order,
    Belo Horizonte, Brazil. 15 August 1971.

80

The Maids.

The first time I put on the black silk panties I got a hardon right away. I felt humiliated in the garter belt. It felt good. I became a prisoner in the high heeled shoes. I had hot and cold flashes. I was delirious. I wanted to bow down and be stepped on. I put on the black uniform of the slave and I was so unbalanced by the sensation of submission that I wanted, needed, to feel Madame's domination to balance me out.

"It is a play about man in the position of a lady's maid." Judith. "It is a play about the class structure. The torture. It is a play about the revolt of the oppressed classes and it is also about their inability to consummate that revolt. They can never stop imitating and wanting to imitate in fact, wanting to be Madame." "*Toujours l'esclave a singé le maitre.*" Proudhon.

When I put on the panties it felt real, and I grooved with it. As if I had taken off the mask instead of having put one on. The pleasures and the humiliation, and all the illusions: that was what I played when I played *The Maids:* the humiliation and illusions of the servant class, the cheap grandeur of the upper class, the cheap grandeur of the illusions, of the swinish mimicry, the corrupt psyche of the Maids and of me and of humankind.

That's why I wanted to play *The Maids* and why I wanted to show it. The play is brilliant: I mean it throws off light, *rayonnante.* You can't play it anymore because the style of theatre in which it is conceived speaks only to the class whose position must be destroyed. Which Genet seeks to destroy. And all of us.

The class for whom *The Maids* was written, the upper classes and their intelligentsia, enthrall the mass not only with Chanel gowns but also with intellectual ballets, *panaches de mots,* waterfalls of words, dazzle, mystification, the whip.

The nature of my attraction to men, to the male body, is sometimes masochistic, sometimes sadistic. I am homosexual up to the waist. Most nights. And down to the neck. The nature of my attraction to women, the female body, is usually erotic; but it is rare that my body responds with the purity of Eros.

Can we not count among the by-products of industrial capital several generations of mechanized, cold, alienated fathers? And could that not account for a psycho-social phenomena: the lost papa people: an aspect of the homosexual syndrome: people looking for, trying to recover, the alienated love of their long lost fathers: the struggle between Eros and the caste system?

Masochism as the link to altruistic love. Judith.

145

In my own quest for reciprocal male love I seek to recover body warmth from the ice age of industry. It becomes part of my revolt. If the relationship is sado-masochist, it is born in some ways out of the feelinglessness of an ice age; and Sadism/Masochism are mechanisms for feeling something, even if it is pain. But feeling the pain, as Artaud conjectured, could open the door to other feelings, which may account for the link between masochism and altruistic love of which Judith speaks. Altruism is revolutionary. As is love.

Feeling like a slave (thru sexual inclinations), the masochist soon identifies with the whole slave class and with (its) suffering: and this evokes altruistic feelings. The act of identification engenders concern for the well-being of the slaves as a class. This leads to revolutionary action which—Genet repeatedly emphasizes—would succeed if the slaves (the Maids) can divest themselves of their schizophrenic desire to play the masters. That's the trick: the work of infusing new pleasures (values) into the culture (the psyche) sexually.

81

Meditations on Theatre II.

The whole theory of Stanislavski was aimed at getting the performer to recreate experience so that it is *almost* existential. The theatre of our time, with its return to ritual and its programme of action is trying to create forms in which alienation from life is changed into integration with life.

Ouro Preto, Brazil. 29 November 1970.

In the work I am doing now I am rebelling even against myself. I push the order of my life into the streets, I let the wall around the art fall, I expose myself to daylight and I look and find that the art is not there, not yet, may never be there, perhaps ought never be there, I feel as if I am creating something I know nothing about, but which I am discovering as I create.

The performer is always afraid to go on stage. Staking your whole life. I am afraid to go out into the streets. Staking your whole life. Buber.

The theatre: a form we have created to help us figure it out, in which we travel to the uncharted isles of mind, body, being.

Croissy-sur-Seine, France. 27 January 1970.

"Poetry makes immortal all that is best and most beautiful in the world." Shelley.

But fifty percent of Whitman's work is subverted by his booby patriotism, his lack of vision in the area of political action, his grotesque war mongering; he fell in with lower level consciousness.

Fifty percent of Shakespeare's work is obviated by his fence sitting, his elegant balance in an unbalanced world, his inability to do ought but augment the structure, his feelinglessness which heralds and proclaims the age of Churchill, and with glorious language he spread the lies, debasing the sacred word with falsehood, no wonder we cry out, "Burn the texts!"

I am aware of the loss of my own blood. Fifty percent of my life . . .

Reggio Emilia, Italy. April 1966. Cefalù, Sicily. March 1968.

Creating *Paradise* in Cefalù—the moment when we realized that it is part of a trilogy of which *Frankenstein* was the Hell, and *Paradise Now* the Purgatory, and that perhaps the next play would be the Paradise. We call it: *The Legacy of Cain,* (after Sacher-Masoch).

Actors/Actresses! Down with Stanislavski! He who cultivated the Art of Acting as the art of characterization: alienation which is our slow death.

The demons, the furies. Help. Hurry. The low buzzing sound. All the time.

São Paulo. 7 January 1971.

Now we are beginning to know that conversation, life itself, is art. The tape recorder changes our concept of the world in a revolutionary manner by supplying a new value which furthers the revolution. Reawakened consciousness of dialogue which is not conversation patterned on the parries of wit. Wit: a barrier. We are no longer interested in winning but in communicating because communication is winning. That is why the media, as McLuhan shows us, are the controlling influence on our behavior. Seize the media: communicate. Control the media, or better, invent them, and you control behavior.

To help the people realize that our lives are art and surpass art, that all men are artists and sublime. Then we may be able to put this genius into our lives. We cannot wait on accident.

San Francisco to Los Angeles. 23 February 1969.

The artist: the antennae of the race. Pound (cited by McLuhan).

It is necessary to stop some things in order to start others. Just as the life of the theatre has to stop in order to remain living. Just as it has to end in order to begin.

Just as I have to end this book which I hold onto the way we do to old ideas or children. Converting life into property, something that you have, *having* instead of *being* (Guy Debord), so I have to end this book, life and contacts that are past, in order to bring the dream into life.

São Paulo. 7 January 1971.

The work of the theatre as the liberation of dreams: the transformation of ideas into working acts.

Porto Alegre, Brazil. 14 February 1971.

82

Meditations 1967-1971 (1930-1971).

Hope exists only in the imagination. We cannot survive without hope therefore we cannot survive without the imagination. This has to do with the work of unleashing the imagination of the people.

Rio de Janeiro. 13 September 1970.

That mixture of darkness and light which is the imagination of the people: the mystery of the imagination is an extension of the universe. And is it possible to imagine what is not real? The universe is mysterious and to the degree that it is mysterious I am a mystic . . . I do not rely on mysterious forces that I do not comprehend but I do not forget that they are to be reckoned with . . .

Modane to Saulieu, France. 4 December 1969.

Then are there demons? . . . Gnosticism: Demonology: the Furies: they possess us all. Who is free? The Furies? No, not even they. Add to all the other problems: none of us is free until we are all free of our demons. Because my demons can get me to thrash out at you. Demons of character, of personality, disposition, ambition, power, revenge, sex, sex demons, sexless demons.

Study demonology. Then the process of exorcism.

Altho I want them to go away, they do not go away. They don't go away because I see them (conscious awareness): they do not disappear in sunlight. They stay, because, like matter, they cannot be destroyed. But they can, like matter, be transformed, but not because you or I will it (want it). They transform into: angels? Angels! The Celestial! When good has been made more interesting than evil. Berdyaev.

Go into that, the way of exorcism.

Brescia, Italy. 24 October 1969.

Releasing the imagination: high language: the truth has to be found here: Coleridge!

The need to kill literature in my life. The linear fascination, my Jewish eyes. Acquisitive: eating of the Tree of Knowledge of Good and Evil, and not, not yet, of the Tree of Life.

Paris. 2 December 1967.

More than ten years now since I started working on this. Writing. I take the fragments of my mind and move them around until something coheres. The demon, he insists that I am too busy living this book to be able to do this.

Judith: Writing—I have to do it in between things; literature—never let it cut into the work.

São Paulo. 6 February 1971.

The youth of our time—the electric generation—is not acting in a play that takes place in three acts on a proscenium stage. They aren't writing their lives that way, they are writing their lives not as characters with little plots, their drama is electric media, planetary in dimension, in tune with cycles and megacycles, the content is new, the form is free from literature, they have within them the knowledge of the Egyptian papyri, the Greek Anthology, without being emotionally attached, for them literature has no demagogues, they do not worship authors the way the Maids in Genet's play worship Madame—to their own undoing; and they are composing a different kind of play, electric, free; and written law will not bind them down. Hope exists in their imagination . . . if it can be freed . . .

Mohammedia, Morocco. 9 July 1969.

Out of what do I come, and this book? . . . Autobiographical references: 1930: my mother who didn't like us to play with guns? 1931: a performance of Humperdinck's *Hansel und Gretel?* Early rhetoric, 1936, to my friends: "I don't fight with my fists!" (I did tho.) Sixteen years old: homosexual intercourse with masochist fantasy. I recognized sex, outside of the limits proscribed by "society," especially with boys and men, as revolutionary. The artist as one who experiments with his own life trying to extend the limits of behavior. The form it took: Bohemianism 1942. 1943: I left Yale, because, like all drop-outs, I could no longer serve that in which I no longer believed whether it call itself my home, my fatherland, or my church. 1943: politics: the American artists' critique of life U.S.A. Pound. 1943: communism: clear then that the democratic-capitalist system was a hoax. 1948: Judith shows me Armand's piece on Individualist Anarchism (reprinted in "Resistance") and we flash out on it; Paul Goodman, guru kept saying, "Anarchism! I'm an anarchist," and explaining it, and 1949 we accepted the basic political and social tenets of anarchism which are still developing all over the planet, anarchism was wiped out by the Stalinists in Spain in the 1930's as it had been wiped out by Trotsky and Lenin in Kronstadt, 1921, and the Ukraine, 1919, but the basic principles have been kept alive and they began reappearing forcefully in the 1960's: the politics and life-style of the new revolutionary generation movement spied the light of the embers, and, feeding them with the breath of their lives, struggle with the establishment socialist and capitalist: toward a free society with food and unconditional liberty for all . . .

The theatre work. What was that? It was always only a vocation, a means of getting there.

Rio de Janeiro. 17 November 1970.

Brazil, December 1970:
Panic. An urgency felt in the belly, fear. It's eighteen days until the first scheduled performance of *Favela Project #1: Christmas Cake for the Hot Hole and the Cold Hole:* the first star in *The Legacy of Cain.*

The Legacy of Cain: conceived as a constellation, with nebulae, red super giants, masses of glowing gas, clusters composed of dozens of stars (in the Hyades, the horns of Taurus: about 150 stars), stars of second magnitude, the Pleiades in the shoulder of Taurus: an open cluster of at least several hundred stars, stars of third and fourth magnitude, and blue dwarfs, belts of asteroids, planetary systems, a constellation that gleams within a city or a village, lingering longer in the cities— maybe two weeks maybe three maybe more, maybe flashing a village for a day or two like a comet.

The whole thing now has been work in progress for months. The work started in Croissy-sur-Seine last winter so it's really almost a year already; and at this point, eighteen days away from it, the *favela* play is not even half finished . . . But it stands on a firm foundation.

As if my whole life had led to this point: the theatre is in the street.

Panic, the urgency felt in the belly. We staged *Antigone* in seventeen days after five months of sitting around discussing it, thirteen to fourteen hours a day rehearsing. This is often done. Adrenalin, the muse.

Most of the work on *Frankenstein,* eleven months of it, was done in the final two months; the final weeks before the Venice and Cassis premieres were ordeals.

We have rushed thru the last weeks of work on every production we have ever done. As if the muse only arrives when terror has struck. Fear of failure? That, too. The boy in Mexico. His silent scream. I work feverishly to appease him.

1949: Judith and I are walking along the streets of Taxco, Mexico. A boy comes up behind us. He is begging for money. We turn. He has no eyes. Sockets with sores, running. I give him all the change that comes out of my pocket. I did not give him all of the money. I gave him all of the small change. And we ran, we ran away from him, but at the same time towards him, towards his millions of doubles.

Judith never let go of an understanding she had at the time: that our work must ultimately aim at wiping out his pain, his poverty, his sickness . . . and their causes. The Taxco oath.

Only now as we prepare the *Favela Project*, only now, 1970, are we turning to face him and his millions of doubles. But we have run so far away. And it is clear to us in the face of the ocean of his suffering that the theatre is only so big . . . Hurry.

Ouro Preto, Brazil. 2 December 1970.

Questions 1969 (II):

Demons. Gnostic interpretations: What is good? What is bad? That is, what is ethics?

How can we organize it?

"Poetry and the principle of Self, of which money is the visible incarnation, are the God and Mammon of the world." Shelley. What is money?

Artaud: "I am a man not completely myself." Of course! Because that's how I want it: I do not want to be myself. Must the Self be transformed, how, before we are ready to liberate ourselves from it? We can't wait that long, there must be a point at which we are sufficiently prepared to go beyond ourselves. What is that point?

When we are all together against the authorities, like Adam and Eve we are for the overthrow of our own immature conceptualization of the universe as a struggle for power. Is there enough time between now and then?

Toulouse, France. May 1969.

"Nothing is easy, no, not getting the food, nor swallowing it, nor keeping it down." Judith.

Never have done anything in the theatre that I have found easy to do. What does this mean?

I don't mean that I have deliberately chosen only difficult things but that it has never been easy. Going out on stage is always difficult. I used to think this was because there was terror of forgetting lines, or stumbling. Humiliation. Too simple an explanation. And I used to think that the terror the performer feels before going on stage was because the audience sitting in the dark was something fearsome, the anonymous brute, the king who sends *lettres-de-cachet* to those who displease him, the madman who slays without reason, the mob that throws rotten eggs and tomatoes, the firing squad, the black robed man who sits in judgment on dais between brass eagle and flag, the shadow. Then I knew that the audience was a lover whom I feared to disappoint. Then the audience became the people on shore to whom the performers returned with messages from outer space: and could they tell them that there is nothing there? or that they didn't get there? or that no one can? Then the hypotheses began to be tested: I began to act in things in which there were no lines to memorize, the lights went up in the house and we met and talked with the audiences, the audiences became people and then individuals and we had dialogue with them. Then they came to throw eggs and tomatoes: in France in the spring of '69 when rightists gave us omelette-finales at performances of *Mysteries* to express their disapproval of what we were doing and saying, and militant minded leftists bombarded the stage with tomatoes and firecrackers to express their rage and disappointment with the fact that we, who bore the imprint of radical thought, who carried the black flag of anarchy, should carry that flag onto the stage of a bourgeois bastion. We, who were saying to a society: "Discard the structure, metamorphose, leave the cocoon, pull yourself out of it"; we were there, still inside the theatres: the students were assaulting us with truth: we had to get out. Hard to do but not so hard that it cannot be done. And what has to be done is hard and I want to make it harder and harder, and the harder it is the easier it is: it has to do with the releasing of energy.

Croissy-sur-Seine, France. 6 March 1970.

"I am in the forest" (Jackson Pollock) "I am in the forest and it is the city and I am painting it." I am in the theatre, and I am making it. I am in the theatre and the theatre is in the street and I am leaving the theatre and entering the street and the theatre is in it and I am going there to make it.

Brussels. 14 December 1969.

The contradiction of my life: the contradiction of this book: this book is the plea of my life to myself, it is me imploring my world, hymn to intellectual beauty, to stop addressing ourselves, onanism, incest, lonely, and henceforth into time, to address the people with the beauty that unfolds enigmas and arouses their lust for life. When this book is over, the two dimensional life among my own class on this one plateau might end, and, rising up, a life of how many dimensions . . . of life against death, union . . .

The contradiction of this book, of my life: the attempt to create (or express) a morality (among other things) that is not bourgeois, when I, and my knowledge, and being, my conditioning are bourgeois. I am he who strives to be traitor to his class, relentlessly, because I have seen the bird of paradise, flying, like summer, heard her singing her fabled song beginning, "The best government is no government. Moult, moult . . ."

Drain (Oregon), U.S.A. 27 October 1971.

83

Avignon, 1968, the year the culture died, we created *Paradise Now*. As we worked on it in the late winter and early spring of that year in the Sicilian town of Cefalù, as we composed the dialectic for a nonviolent anarchist revolution, we were already part of the movement which flowered all over the world that year, and in France in May. *Zeitgeist*.

Compelled by the here and now to withdraw from the Festival, we had no heart to go on with it, we saw that it was in fact the counter-revolution, all these festivals.

All art began to disappear that year, all the beautiful art that we have all treasured, all the art which we believed was a form of maximal type experience. That year we began to see art as that which makes the structure strong. All that festival art making its privileged audiences believe that the sight of the face of God is imminent in a Festival product. Now the sight of the face of God is always imminent for anyone who looks, as it is said. But to be looking means that you cannot be hiding. "Adam hides himself to escape responsibility for his life, he turns existence into a system of hideouts. And in this hiding again and again from 'the face of God,' he enmeshes himself more and more deeply in perversity." Buber. When one hides from the people, one hides from the face. When you stare at art, festivals, where the people cannot come because they are alienated from the spot for economic, social, or cultural reasons, it is a way of hiding from God.

Two specific incidents gave us the excuse we needed to withdraw from the Festival. The first was the prohibition of further performances of *Paradise Now* (we were asked to substitute *Antigone*); and the second was the prohibition of free performances in the streets of Avignon. (The night before we made our declaration withdrawing from the Festival, we had been met by seventy five well-armed policemen when we went into the workers' quarter at Champfleury to give a free performance of *Mysteries* in the streets.) But in the declaration we drew up we wanted to make the real reasons for our action clear. We gave eleven reasons, and, right in the middle, reasons numbers six and seven said that we were withdrawing because:

> 6.   You cannot serve God and Mammon at the same time, you cannot serve the people and the state at the same time, you cannot tell the truth and lie at the same time . . .

7. The time has come at last for us to begin to refuse to serve those who do not want the knowledge and power of art to belong to any but those who can pay for it, who wish to keep the people in the dark, who work for the Power Elite, who wish to control the life of the artist and the lives of the people.

After '68, the culture dead in the breast, the international conspiracy went to work. We are looking for other ways out of the labyrinth, we have no maps, and the Minotaur (Mammon) lurks behind each corner and as we steal along the corridors repeating the mantra "Venceremos . . . venceremos . . ." we find ourselves, October 1970, creeping thru the jungle of it in Rio de Janeiro: Where? What? How? Uneasy circumstances, unaccustomed problems, a different terrain. Crossing the class barriers fills me with a kind of fear, I sweat, twisting my fingers: I think that it is the feeling of inadequacy among the workers, the Lumpenproletariat, the peasants, the marginals, the poorest of the poor, I don't know them, I have no fluid language in which to talk to them. Am unequipped!

Worse: I fall asleep at night slipping into nostalgic reverie about the years we travelled thru Europe in VW buses, stoned, looking at the landscape, barely getting by, but getting by all the time, and I remember theatres where appreciative audiences received us and thanked us. "Nostalgia is reactionary . . ."

Now all the certainty is gone. Nothing fits together anymore, everything is a little out of place, says Joe Chaikin . . .

Fortunately. I *know* this. But I do not yet *feel* it. I am now un-illusioned. Good. But I am also uncomfortable; this journey is not a theatrical tour. The bourgeois structure dispenses comfort for a limited number of people, creature comfort, intellectual comfort. And in order to be comfortable that way, alienation is necessary. So an alienating culture is created, in which it is possible to demi-comprehend everything and do nothing about it, to have intellectual/cultural solace, to bear the unbearable, to live a short life and to die. The comfortable road to death.

Maybe in order to live, like paleolithic man trying to figure it out, in all discomfort, the tools are found. "Liking" has nothing to do with it. Neither does the person who makes the cloth for my coat (Marx) "like" the job. Now the garment worker will never get to like it until the whole structure changes. But I always remain privileged; I am always doing what I want to do, even when I don't like it.

Crawling on my belly thru the *favelas* of Rio, in the muck and shit, scared, tentative, unsure, the wind raging about me, night, I find myself sensing something I have never before sensed, I ask myself what it is, it is hard to identify because it is so new, but my heart pounding pounds it out: this strange feeling is a sense of strength, and the fear that I fear is not weakness—in the past, in my security and growing fame there was only really growing weakness—the fear is the fright that comes with an awareness of strength, and for the first time in my life I begin to realize that in the past the culture, the way of life, was always draining me, making me weaker even as it gave me medals and comfort, but now I am experiencing the transition from down to up, from illusion to power.

Rio de Janeiro. 11 October 1970.

84

Document: Eric Gutkind on What Is To Be Done

1.

"The Messianic movement is now with Marx and not with Jesus."

2.

" 'Man is the Messiah of nature.' Novalis. God has a worldly destiny."

3.

"God is absent because we are absent."

4.

"Real change will not come from politics but philosophy."

5.

"Ritual always does 'letting-free'."

6.

"The new *Zimzum* ('letting-free') is delegated by God to Man. Man answers. He responds to the *Zimzum*, withdrawing from the three 'nothings' or three 'itnesses' (images, powers, things), and goes back to his own 'essence,' his own 'destiny.' It is unfettered. Every form of owning, power and privilege is the strongest and most effective form of ontic perversion. Therefore a genuine revolution, in its profoundest sense, would be a ritual pattern."

7.

"The Ritual of sacrifice was a saying NO to the 'havable,' an act of letting-free (*Zimzum*). The new letting-free (*Zimzum*), the new breaking-up (*Shevirah*), the new primal choice (*Kissutz*), is the true demarcation line."

8.

"The ritual is the raising of all our faculties to the maximum and enables us to live with maximal intensity. The dammed-up and collected physical strength of the people is almost limitless. It focuses the midst."

9.

"In the realm of nature there are no ethics, only might. Nature is without mercy. Ethics is exclusively the law of mankind."

10.

"Man is the freedom of the universe, of nature. He can transcend himself."

11.

"In genuine communion HE would emerge. The fear man has is the fear of HIS emerging."

12.

"The Way—the Jump—There!! Suddenness is the hope, rather than evolution."

13.

"The great new step is the letting-free (Zimzum) of Man!"

14.

" 'Above and beyond' is no *heaven*; there is only Man rising ever higher."

15.

"The abandonment of the Ego-Self: the abandonment of Capital and the State."

16.

"Holiness (Kadosh) means 'raised above,' 'lifted free.' "

85

"A spectre is haunting Europe
the world
We call him Comrade."
— Rafael Alberti: *Spain, 1936.*

"The verbal delirium of intellectuals."
— Luis Mercier Vega: *Roads to Power in Latin America.*

Utopian rhetoric, to put an end to it by fulfilling it.

Utopian rhetoric, utopian poetry, the utopian dream in fact, like the eternal woman (inspiration), they draw us always on.

Now as long as the economy remains a money economy, authoritarian procedures (from the shop steward to President of the Corporation, or even President of the Republic) will be required.

In fact money has so thoroly corrupted us that people imagine authoritarian procedures are necessary in order to distribute things fairly. Breaking out of the limits of money's myths: the work of the revolutionist.

There is a point at which the fulfillment of desire, as well as needs, must be recognized because sanity and the imagination hang dependent.

The race: money and authority keep getting stronger at the same time that the revolutionaries keep increasing and getting stronger. We are racing a mechanized computer: the "Frankenstein Monster" we have created to solve all our problems—and this "Frankenstein Monster" does in fact control us. But this monster deteriorates as it grows. The question is whether we can survive its death in which it threatens to bring everything down with it.

Utopian rhetoric is imploring and encouraging us to get out of the industrial revolution trap; utopian poetry tries to change consciousness, never letting us forget the hunger, but telling us to go beyond survival, beyond even the successes of socialism: total revolution. The utopian dream unifies our objectives.

The uses of hyperbole: not to invent new forms but to hasten new birth. The intention of utopian rhetoric: to move people off their asses and into work, to liberate ourselves from contradictions and new contradictions as they occur: verbal shock: stimulation:

then, at the moment of overstimulation: suspend treatment: take recourse to subtler devices: the process will go thru many phases in the coming decades: learning to vary the strategy: to be quicker than, to outwit, the lugubrious monster:

to recognize the moment to go underground:

and when to emerge.

Bologna, Italy. 5 November 1969.

86

This book, this examination: it is to find out if it is true that everything conceived in terms of theatre, and in terms of the needs of our time, can be tuned, scalpeled, twisted, pressed, squeezed until it declares its affinity with the revolutionary proposals of anarchism and violentless human relations. I examine and I see the forces gathering: the *Zimzum:* that most tremendous event when the Creator Spirit withdrew himself from all human beings—SETTING US FREE—so that we could indeed be free to create ourselves: free, we have chosen chains out of psychological perversion; but free we can free ourselves also. The Creator Spirit sets us free by relinquishing control, the position of leader, of authority, of government. The example of this divine action is the soul of anarchism. Thus anarchy (freedom) equals violentless (non-coercive) human relations.

Aix-en-Provence to Avignon, France. 16 May 1970.

87

Enumeration, enumerative poetry, the linear eye, Solomon, Whitman, Breton, Rimbaud, Pound, Lorca, Smart, Ginsberg, the linear mind, McLuhan, adding it up, Pascal, Stein, Guy Debord, their books add it up, numerology, the linear focus, the list, the lists of my life, laundry lists, grocery lists, lists of plays seen, music heard, books read, lists of things to do, day after day, hour after hour, this is how I live, I put it all together in the plays, in the action, *Paradise Now* is linear, ten rungs, a vertical ladder with horizontal wings, this book for instance strings it all out, like a road to walk on, thru a city, a maze, turn after turn, back thru the same street at a different time in a different light and out again, finding the way, block after block, the road in fact that I have walked for ten years, this book, for my whole life, I am in the forest, I walk from tree to tree, stone past stone, birds, ferns, faces, flies, jobs, beds, beggars, radios, water sellers, mines, cafes, lathes, dressing rooms, events, morgues, all details preserved, adding it up. Where there is form it all fits together. But my life, which is in this list of words, this book, I don't see the form, only accruing, acquisition, greed, things, day to day, experience after experience, this is how I go from face to face, my way, my reality, pilgrim's progress, my Book of Numbers.

Finally, I think it becomes circular, spherical, global; i.e., universal. When a moment is not a step between the last and the next, when counting disappears, and you exist in it, radiating back and forth in all dimensions, out of history, escape from time as door that is opening and closing second by second. I see myself now and I ask you to see me as an agent of Death, conditioned by Death, living my life dying, life a thing that passes from thing to thing, absorbing and excreting, growing, changing, adding, and subtracting-by-forgetting. I am waiting for it to come together, no Act I, II, III, only the present action.

I wait for the moment when adding it up is no longer the compulsion. Is it possible only when the problems of life are no longer arithmetical? Mathematics never stops. I am waiting for solid geometry. Physics.

Three dimensional life is the privilege of the privileged. When there is no hunger, then one meal does not lead only to the next, life flowers in all directions, it does not hoard, it has, it produces, it reproduces, it survives, it confronts the multidimensional. Maybe I count in order to see if I am walking or standing still.

In one of the Chinese operas which Judith and I saw performed by the Sun Opera Company in a theatre under the Manhattan Bridge in New York in 1950, a giant mechanical cardboard lotus slowly opened on the stage, it took forty five minutes while the actress, crouched in the matrix, sang and sang, slowly rising and spreading, her sleeves slowly unwinding, the arms slowly extending, never taking a step, the thigh muscles slowly elevating the body as the body of the lotus bloomed. Time passed, note after note, word after word she sang, because she was the Golden Flower, and I can understand my life only as a process of becoming, and I see the whole of society that way, counting our blessings, reciting our sins, trying to unfold petal by petal.

When I was a child I believed that people lived to be a hundred and then died.

In school they made it so that one hundred was the ultimate number, perfect, if you got one hundred on a test then you knew everything. I am counting the sinister passage of time.

In India, Mann points out, you ask a man how old he is and he answers, around fifty five.

How many acts are there in it, how many angels can dance on the head of the pin, when are there enough people to take the necessary action, how many do we need to overthrow capitalism and the state, to get on with it. Counting the strokes of the hours, counting, the sexual act.

Miscounting.

Rio de Janeiro, Belo Horizonte, Brazil.
11 October — 19 July 1971.

88

I work. Nothing happens. I work. Nothing happens. What did I eat today, how's my head, is it burned out, is it wet, am I distracted because C has gone away, or J is dead? What are the conditions for the creative event?

The question: What are the best conditions for the creative event?

The answer: Shaving? Shitting? Riding in the subway? Falling asleep in the middle of a conversation about the murder of Ben Barka, or about *The Who*, or about how to do a play about the sinking of Venice? Or, while droning out for the 606th time the fundamental information, unheralded, mysterious, like birds, remember, the creative idea flies into the head. John Cage.

No strict guide to what produces the creative breakthru. A physical function we know little about. Theta waves? Until we can increase our cerebral capacity, it isn't likely that we will know what force it is that thru the green fuse drives the flower.

I rehearse, I perform, sometimes it swings, sometimes it doesn't. Seeking formulae so that it's always high, always happening. Who knows? No one. How beautiful *not* to know: limitation limitless: the secret of life:

creativity. We don't know much more than that it has to do with entering a state of ever-presence. Ever present engagement in the pursuit. What makes it yield, what attracts the muse, the Creator Spirit, what precipitates the creative act, the heroic moment? Ever-present concentration on the pursuit so that everything you do including eating, sex, and reading comics are involved with, relate to, the problem. Like a long pregnancy. And the process does not have to be conscious. If the metaphysical obsession is great enough, it comes when you least expect it.

Do not shut out the unknown.

How else can we hope to solve the problem of creating the theatrical event that will move the people to burn down the slums and occupy the Ritz? Everything revolves around that question: there is no other emergency.

They say that they used to teach Latin and Algebra in the schools with the idea that it trained the mind to think (linear). This has something to do with the assumption that there is a linear formula that leads to the creative event, but now we know that it can come from any direction. You have to be like a bell, hanging in space, open and susceptible to the wind, the impulse whenever it comes and from whichever direction, ready to ring.

This is the crux of it: when the mind is open to the impulse, to the Creator Spirit, it receives it and transmits it. Holy condition. When the community is open to it, it recognizes it collectively, seizes it and works with it.

When the people are ready for the revolution, waiting, hoping, concentrating, invoking, obsessed, ever-present in the seeking, then the event will happen. This is what we Jews mean when we say that the Messiah will come when everyone is weeping—or praying—or laughing. And no one can calculate ahead of time, with a linear formula, just when that will be. No one knows when the thief in the night, Bakunin's, will come.

Bong, clang, and we cross the line.

Croissy-sur-Seine, France. 27 January 1970.

89

Techniques of Confrontation Politics:
New York City, March 1969:

The Living Theatre   X   "The Theatre of Ideas":
The Insupportability of the Intellectual's Comfort:
What is Detachment?   What is Passion?   What is Love?:
What is Passivity?   What is Action?
Where Are We at?

The night that we, The Living Theatre, trashed the established form for polite intellectual discourse, boils burst. You would have thought the inner dome of heaven had fallen in. The shattering of illusion? No. Not yet. Not enough.

Shirley Broughton had organized a series of forums for intellectual discussion of specific issues. It consisted of bringing together an elite, a 'peer group,' more or less, in two parts.

The first part consisted of a group of about three speakers, experts, presumably qualified to discuss the topic, talking for about an hour; and the second part consisted of a question period. On the night that I am talking about, this audience maintained its exclusivity by paying a significantly large entrance fee ($10) for the privilege of gathering and of engaging in talk, not about technical matters, but rather about aesthetic issues. Not ideology. And not revolution. And always reform. Usually reform of outlook. To increase the playground area, the limited area, where the intellect can comfortably measure limited aspects of problems and questions that affect the small ground on which the intellectual stands and lives out his life, and plays, and eats.

In this circumstance we tried to extend the games of the intellect to include confrontation with physical and emotional NEED. The intellectuals, secure in their class, are always safe from starving (even if they sometimes hope and pray for a little check in payment for poem or article). Their class will ultimately protect them from the more vicious forms of exploitation, so that they are simply cut off from a realistic sense of urgency. The sense of urgency is always paralyzed by the natural tendency of the mind to temporize, to nourish itself on scruples, to postpone action, in fact to be so divorced from life as to have a horror of action. Clinging to, gobbling up the Tree of Knoweldge, paying no mind to the Tree of Life, intellectuals have a horror of emotion, and recoil from the central problems by toying artfully with contradictions. No wonder Hamlet is their favorite play. In it they see themselves elevated to hero, "the tragedy of a man who could not make up his mind."

Impotence thru intellectualization: the body (life itself) becomes inactive.

We are trying to put the intelligence and energy of the intellectual at the service of the people. To locate the intellectual among the people. Where the Creator Spirit dwells. In the Midst. Gutkind.

From Passive to Active. Activity needed now.

To what degree does the intellectual (philosophy) influence the people?

The thing about Lenin, says Judith, was that he got it together. Is it possible for state socialism not to inhibit the free production of art and expression? Is it possible for capitalist democracy not to inhibit the mind?

The circumstances: At "The Theatre of Ideas" that night it was a benefit for the theatre. That's why it cost so much to get in; but there was whiskey; people have paid ten dollars and more to see a Living Theatre play, and that's just as bad. It was happening at the Quaker Meeting House, a public landmark, we've played in many, off Gramercy Park, and the catchy theme was 'Theatre or Therapy?', Nat Hentoff moderating, and the speakers: Paul Goodman, Robert Brustein, Judith Malina and Julian Beck. What level of life do we move on, how many at a time?

So we broke it up. Spontaneously. Rufus, Jenny, Henry, Steve Israel, Steve Thompson, Pierre Biner, they made a total improvisation. This, the truth, was doubted by many. Because the intellectual can't even conceive of spontaneity. Lenin too had difficulty with the concept of spontaneity, he wanted it controlled, and the system he inaugurated is still severely controlled. The influence of the intellectual on the popular culture in a system like capitalism has a repressive effect. The paradox is that it ought to stimulate action but all it keeps stimulating is intellectual action, it rationalizes urgency into something that time will look after if the human mind just keeps developing; it fails to precipitate the only thing that can ultimately redeem it: action, by the people.

We were also conducting a direct action lesson in the understanding of spontaneity.

It got to be like a collective trance. The loud sound of people talking to each other, many in anger, makes you talk louder and this leads to ranting, and when you're ranting you're in trance. Possessed. And thru the symbols that erupt in anger the great spirit sometimes pours.

I made it tough for them to justify what I was doing. I tore hat coat glasses off woman, shrieking: "The weight of your furs makes it impossible for the needs of the people to touch you!" I threw things all over the room, put human relationship in crisis. "I despair of the intellectual ever really taking part in the real revolution when it comes to it. We walk around its edges. I despair of myself!"

We, The Living Theatre, were accused of falling into fascism because what we did was looked on as the disruption of the democratic process, as not exercising emotional constraint, as using physical violence— throwing a woman's coat across a room, tearing it from her back! A woman! Eyeglasses! Pocketbook! Private possessions! I battered my way with sound thru the wall between us, I railed against property, I cried out my despair, despair that we could ever touch or love each other, or even adequately communicate. But the vascillating intellectual confuses this with fascism. "Call the police!" they cried, because the intellectuals aren't hungry.

And aren't oppressed. And like the bourgeoisie which they are, they always have recourse to calling the police, and, as Durutti says, when they feel their backs against the wall, they do in fact take recourse to fascism.

The intellectuals speak with vigor about their need for intellectual freedom but fail to achieve it most of the time because they can't take action; they keep addressing their own class, at best hoping that some of the 'light' will seep down, downwards, by itself into the lower classes.

The intellectuals at 'The Theatre of Ideas' all adore Artaud, but when we turned their symposium into a Theatre of Cruelty in which they themselves experienced outrage, anger, lies, hysteria, irrationality, rage, vehemence, sputum, the edge of physical violence, and trance, they backed right out.

Maybe the institutional forms have to be destroyed: then the intellectuals will be free to extend themselves. Maybe then they will be more disposed to their own emotions. The pit of the stomach, the pelvis, there where feeling is felt, the genitals, where there is hunger and pain, is the way in, the door of entry. And then, sensitized to the pain, maybe they will take the actions that can cure the malady now that it has been located. This small chance may be the intellectuals' only way to free their limited self, their limited life, from limited use into transcendence.

The subject of this is the cultural revolution. We have to recognize that no one, no one will be untouched by the revolution. We have to get ourselves into a condition in which we flow with it so that we survive this inevitable period of transformation, this scientifically inevitable event.

Rigidity will crack, dry twigs snapping in the tempest now brewing on the hot table lands, the arid wastes, inevitable the great winds coming. No longer cling to the dry stalks, our antiquated biological forms, we have to free ourselves as seeds, making ourselves available to the elemental upheaval, so that the west wind can do its work.

Wind: the rushing of air to fill a vacuum. The vacuum created by the inbreath of the people, suffocating, gasping for air.

Rio de Janeiro. 3 November 1970.

90

Woodstock Nation: the Hippie Love Rock Life Style Music Revolution. The establishment encourages it: it has buying power. Abbie makes that clear in his book: the establishment encourages it in order to encompass it and exploit it economically.

Time, Life, & Newsweek praise dope (soft stuff), praise the life-love style, praise the music, and the beads and customs.

Woodstock Nation frees the children of the bourgeoisie from the bourgeois form of life.

But it does not free the worker who manufactures the records or the guy who harvests the weed, or the farmer who gathers the eggs for all the egg-salad, the person who harvests the malt for the beer and the milk-shakes.

Nor is the example of the drop-out of the bourgeois daughter/son from the bourgeois cage encouraging. "You can't live if you don't have money!" Everybody knows this; and it is clear to the laborer breaking rocks in the street that the alternative life style of Woodstock Nation lives off the cake crumbs of Capital's table.

The Woodstock rebellion doesn't free the Third World, the uneducated Brazilian peasants from their Aluminum Corporation of America master. It doesn't make them revolt. They just look on, if they see us at all with their tired eyes, enviously.

This is the revolution which—as long as it abjures political and social action—supports the system just as the system supports it.

The wailing of the people will soon drown out the sound of this music. But then it will be too late. And the sound of the wail increases as the repression grows stronger. And the wars will go on because protest and sentiment will not topple the system that can contain protest and sentiment and go on doing just what it wants to do.

The more technocratically advanced the system within geographical limitations (I am talking about nations as sociological entities), and the richer the entity the more easily it can contain and control. Therefore the more successful the capitalist system, the more formidable it is in its subtle supple strength, tho the enormity of its mass makes cracks in its foundation.

Sing. Dance. Love. Peace. Get High. Graze. Flip out. Trip. Free Yourselves. Do your own thing. The revolution of individual expression that divests itself of bourgeois attributes while continuing citizenship in the capitalist world is not sufficient for the needs of this planet.

This revolution, this hedonism, exploits gently while capitalist democracy exploits ruthlessly. Is that how to do it?

Woodstock Nation: Superior Product of Bourgeois Culture.

It is all privilege. Privilege means classes. Dig it.

Up against the wall, Woodstock Nation! The hungry are pointing their guns. At us. The Aristocratic Poets of the Bourgeois Party.

Woodstock Nation does the beautiful Bacchus dance while the Apollonians rule and reek.

If Woodstock Nation doesn't attack the economic, social, and political machinery with the same force with which it transforms the products of that machinery, it's just an exceptional child, a genius, a prodigy, like Mozart, who played for the king all the time.

Just as Mozart or the rebellious Joyce and Beardsley were the offshoots and continuation of the Golden Civilization.

My job is to tell you this, to goad. Because I know who I am and who you are, and I know what you and I can do.

I am prophet and I see the Golden Doom, the carbonated blood, disaster, the thrilling fucking, the cosmic consciousness that knows all about the Andromeda Galaxy but doesn't hear the sobbing across Africa, the whimpering in coked Peru, because in its revulsion at the world of money and the state, it has recoiled from the revolution of action.

That's why Woodstock Nation is a soft bet for *Life Magazine*.

Because the forces of repression can tolerate changes in life style: the history of art, for instance, is the history of revolutions in style that are first rejected and then accepted.

Look to it.

"I have murdered your father. I have murdered your mother. Now, look to it."

They are murdering our brothers. Now, look to it.

Because all the gorgeous beauty of our life-style will be wiped away either by:

1.   The demonic rage of a wounded capitalism
or

2.   The blood bath that will come when the holy monster THE PEOPLE rises up, untouched by our nonviolent vibrations, by our songs sung while they crawled to work, bleeding in the factories, pulsing in the hot wet marshes where the rice and mosquitoes live, while they lurched and quarreled with each other in the shit infested ghetto lands battling lice, fleas, rats.

We're so fucking aware, so turned on, so tuned in, so beautiful, so holy in our hopes and ways.

"I have set before you life and death: choose."

It is clear, is it not, what *Life Magazine* is?

Avaloketesvera: "I will not leave the torture garden until everyone gets out."

But no one gets out until we all do really: because we are tied together by the magic of it all, our love for one another, our interdependence, the mutual life flow.

If we are an unhappy people it is not only because of our individual hassles and hangups. For proof: turn on the light in the collective unconscious.

It is time to turn on all the lights. Turn on all the lights in this world-box-theatre we are in, so that not one single shred of phony mystery remains. Then, in the light of action, let us dance our way out O Woodstock Nation.

Arezzo, Italy. 19 November 1969.

172

91

The Occupation of the Odéon. Part I.

It was important to occupy the Odéon just because it was *le Théatre de France* where the government gave the Barrault-Renaud Company the chance to do Beckett and Adamov and Ionesco and Genet. Genet! Because the students and their comrades were refusing in May 1968 to grant the government the privilege of flattering both itself and the public into believing that the state maintains reputable avant-garde *contra-sistemo* art. Any art that the establishment supports it exploits, any art that the establishment supports is already infected. So powerful the germs of corruption. We are fighting a plague. The occupation of the Odéon represented the attempt to occupy one of the mechanisms of co-option.

It was important to find a vivid device to show that we know that any art made for the privilege of one class (those who can pay the price to get in) works against the other classes. We do not grant the bourgeoisie the privilege of sharpening their wits on Genet and Beckett at the expense of the poor who are deprived of proper alimentation for the proper biological growth of the brain as well as of basic social and cultural necessities.

It was important to say that the theatres—even the best of their kind— ought to be at the service of the people where the people could gather not to watch the lives of their mythic superiors acted out, but to play out ritually the drama of the revolution, each spectator there to participate in planning and creating the revolutionary changes that might alter the cosmos.

A theatre for the person in the street is more meaningful than a theatre to house Shakespeare, Claudel, Gide, and Genet. All power to the people.

What took place the night of May 15, 1968, inside the Odéon was the most beautiful thing I have ever seen in a theatre.

The occupation of the Odéon had all the elements of great theatre: a cast of vivid characters, great poetic tirades, conflict of ideas, the clash of potent ideologies, a reality surpassing the contrivances of dramatists, the emergence of the people as the hero, and the end which came a month later as awkward tragedy with the invasion of the police, tragic like the whole story of France in May, like Spain, like Kronstadt, like all the great anarchist dramas.

The essence of tragedy: just when the hero knows it all, the he and the she of it, the in and the out, the truth, just when he is most ready to live, to act, he dies, stabbed by civilization, unnecessary victim of our artificial fate.

The Occupation of the Odéon. Part II.

in a fink revolution the *folies bergère* is taken
and made to play ionesco
in a fascist *coup d'état* the *comédie francaise* can't play
           antigone or *the bacchae*
in a socialist revolution in france the experiments of
         barrault would be encouraged because they would mean
         prestige at home and abroad
but a political position would always have to be veiled

but what was happening in france in may 1968
was not a revolution against stalinism
it was a revolution against kapital
         and its beneficent poses

The French Revolt of 68 shook everyone up because the idol of the West—France—capitalism's finest showpiece (finer than the U.S. because more 'cultured')—was being contested by its own citizens, its own people were crying out and acting. They were saying
we want the miracle: paradise now!
and they dreamed that it would happen
and they tried to bring the dream into being . . .

11,000,000 on strike in a country of 50,000,000—and it was clear that for everyone on strike there were 2-3 sympathetic persons in addition — more than half the country was high, really high, on the idea that the miracle of miracles was going to happen: that after it was over the life of injustice and degradation would be past and that a new phase of human development would begin.

174

With deep sorrow everyone came to know that we, the people, were not prepared. But everyone, including the police, and the ministers, let it go on as long as they could because each human unconscious wanted the *deus-ex-machina*, the impossible, to arrive; that an unprepared France could suddenly divest itself of capitalism avoiding the crippling diseases of State Socialism, and become a communal productive society in which all would give and receive according to their power and their need.

The theatre of that spring in France was the most elevating and intoxicating thing the French people of this century had experienced: they were acting, acting great roles.

It was clear in the Odéon. The drama was in the auditorium, not on the stage, but in the theatre where the spectators had become the protagonists and were playing the Tribune of the Revolution, a great drama in 30 days. Every terrible speech which lasted half an hour of bored listening was of more importance in the history of our immortal souls and mortal bodies than the great celebrated tirades of Racine and Corneille.

These dramas were written in the Book of Life. Amen.

The role-playing: everyone was in a trance and in the trance acting a divine play of holy authorship, dizzily impelled towards their own liberation. The theatrical elements in the culture were providing patterns for action, great improvisation. Life became important, each moment vivid, high, not tired debauched drama, but up there, beyond the death ritual.

São Paulo, Brazil. 19 August 1970.

92

The Genius of the People. I used to think that genius was an individual trait. Restricted. The genius of the people of India to insist on making living into a spiritual adventure, their understanding of process. The genius of the Chinese people to mass together to end five thousand years of suffering. The genius of the Jewish People (not as nation) who recognize the need to sanctify life thru ritual, the constant recreation of holiness, the genius of yearning for unification, evoking the presence of God.

Marx & Aeschylus. Marx ascribes the birth and growth of the bourgeoisie and of bourgeois democracy to the mercantile rage against feudalism. The bourgeoisie performed a revolutionary function but the bourgeoisie no longer has a revolutionary function hsitorically. The bourgeoisie has been undone by the power they gained, the form of life they chose. Absorbed by the things they desired, they themselves have become a thing, they are no longer the people, but rather a stone on top of the people, to be overthrown. Marx was concerned with the creation of the people.

How can I tell you that I wish you no harm, O Middle Class, I must love you with the love force, *Ahimsa* of all my being. Your children (the people of Woodstock Nation) are telling you, listen, abandon your fears . . .

Where have we come from? Where are we? The ideals of the bourgeoisie have disappeared in the desert we've made of the land. The polluted planet. The worker, he doesn't even want freedom anymore. He wants to be free to make as much money as possible. The syndrome of the Golden Calf.

Vestiges of the bourgeois thing: You have free speech but you can be sure that all the media of communication are controlled by the elite. Goodman. The United States has the Declaration of Independence and the Bill of Rights. They serve only to mask the reality of our bondage.

You cannot be a Christian inside a capitalist structure. Jesus drove the money changers out of the temple. But now we know that the whole world is the temple. Now we know that we cannot finally come together as the people as long as money divides us. Aeschylus: There is a chorus and there is a protagonist. But each member of the chorus is the protagonist in his own life, a drama equally fabulous, equally beautiful, and less covered with royal guilt and death-murder.

The chorus always speaks the great words of the drama, expresses the great wisdom.

The form of the play, however, is such that the spectator can never really know this.

Aeschylus is the culture of the Hero and the Mass. Democracy and fascism proclaim this boldly. Socialism does this sinisterly.

Assault on the culture. What is missing in Aeschylus is the full concept of the organism: the genius of the people is subordinated – that old error – to individual power of aristocrats. But holiness, GOD (incontestable genius), dwells in the People. Which Marx knew.

Milan. 1 November 1969.

93

The view that people are bad (the concept of the Fall of Man) and that therefore we have to have law and government and money is not the view of the people but of the ruling class, foisted on us by a corrupt priesthood to maintain the elite and their priests in their position of power.

If, as Gandhi says, capital engenders greediness and competitiveness as character traits, might anarcho-communism engender generosity and cooperation? The theory of the revolution is not based on the idea that human character is "good," but that if we change the conditions in which we function, our character will change.

Detention Cells. D.O.P.S. (Department of Political and Social Order). Belo Horizonte, Brazil. 16 August 1971.

94

The re-structure will not happen
        led by leaders and groupuscules.
Restructure can only mean:
        created by all
        the people.

The essential work: build the mass movement.

The essential of our work is the building of a MASS movement.

The essential work is to build a mass movement.

We have to build a mass movement.

Our work is to build a mass movement.

Croissy-sur-Seine, France. 15 February 1970.

95

How to build a mass movement?

Where does the revolutionary vanguard come from? The contradiction: from the declassé intellectuals (usually enlightened bourgeoisie), not from the proletariat, not from the poor, not from the landless masses. To this enlightenment the theatre as we know it has made a substantial contribution. It has helped to bring those members of the bourgeoisie who are in-the-process-of-enlightenment to the realization that even what is enlightening them must be transformed: because the process which served for them is too slow for the mass which is bursting like bags of blood under the weight of the structure.

To build a mass movement:
What can the theatre do? Release the creative impetus into the people.
Change the atmosphere. Change the moral values. Change perception.
Change the mode of thought. Change the music. Go down into Egypt.
To the slaves. What can the theatre do? It can entice, zap, pull, inform,
cajole, and openly inspire the proletariat, the Lumpenproletariat, the
poor, the poorest of the poor.

What can the theatre do?
It can provoke
the need and the desire.
It can unchain
the energy compressed under the weight
of the pyramidal structure
egypt
so that the bottom moves
upwards.

The rest then happens
more or less spontaneously.

Cannes, France. 14 May 1970.

96

Meditation. 1988.

Marks twenty years of struggle. The technocratic society consolidating
its power. The major interest, comrade Roszak points out, of those who
lavishly finance research is weapons, techniques of social control. Control: the spirit flags under the eerie devices, surveillance, internal espionage: no government trusts its people.

Sinister: the adjective describes everything. Good. Nothing is left anymore except vertical thrust of rebellion. Darkness reigns downward. We

send pilot lights, slim shafts, laser beams, upwards. Open contestation no longer possible anywhere. The authorities want

strict control of the mind of man.

The first work of the revolutionary: to keep his own mind free.

The struggle continues.

We have our secret ways. Human ways. To the slaves in the mines and the fields we bring bread and poetry. Can they forbid bread?

97

Meditation. 1998.

Clefts in the tundras! The foundation! the steel state is cracking, the money machine is grinding to a halt, the noise is fearsome. Malignant tumors, the accumulation of "large blobs," predicted a hundred and twenty five years ago by the doctors Marx, Bakunin, Freud. The plague: Artaud's "breakdown of the social structure." The mass suffers from the famines of Malthus. The whisper is "new morning": the weathervane points to clean sweep. The upper classes: giant mental ward: require special care. The mass is amassing energy to make love (Goodman) "to fuck their only world."

Death itself, the underground biologists report, is only a disease! A state of mind! New winds, changing values.

"Who has ever *seen* that hydrogen and oxygen combine to make water?" (Gutkind's question.) No one has yet seen what is bursting from our vines, our fingers, pushing up towards the light, new morning, *la lutte continue.*

98

Meditation. 2008.

ecstasy enters the masses . . . first phase of anarchic eras . . .

"Fact is no longer that which is most certain, it has become the most enigmatic." (E. Gutkind, prophet.)

work, work on what has been spoiled, putting together the split mentality . . . do you think it less difficult now than it used to be? it is not less difficult. but less painful, less sorrowful, life is not a sordid drama anymore.

the struggle . . . *la lucha* . . . *continua* . . . as we prepare . . . we are preparing . . . for the return . . . into our souls . . . our midst . . . of . . . long exiled . . . joy . . .

99

Meditation. 1970.

Bah. Down in the mouth. When personal relations weaken the body, shatter the spirit. We spend our lives living down the tempers we are born with. Stein. If there is no peace between friends, how can there be peace in the world. Pound. I talk of the masses, of revolution, but what of personal love? Bah. Down in the mouth.

So much of poetry and philosophy always saying, "Find yourself first." Yoga and Tantra hung there. Sure I must find myself, but I surely won't if I don't find you, and I won't find you if I don't bring down the bully state, to which I, I the anarchist, am nevertheless a slave. I won't find joy in the free society until I am divested of my neuroses, my morbid particles. We can never (Freud) be free of the neurotic inclinations in this booby society. None of us is free until we are all free, all or nothing, that's the only reality. Utopia. Paradise now. Love is perfection.

Anybody who doesn't suffer doesn't feel. Anybody who isn't sad is doped by lies. Consciousness of suffering will turn the key ... part way.

Croissy-sur-Seine, France. 7 June 1970.

100

Bomb Culture. Jeff Nuttall. In 1945 the sound changed. Millennial Apocalyptic Fears and Visions taken on common sense as year 2000 approaches.

From the *Brazil Herald* (published in Rio de Janeiro):

> "Washington (UPI) October 15, 1970—Communist China and the Soviet Union exploded multi-megaton nuclear devices an hour and one-half apart yesterday the Atomic Energy Commission reported. The Russian blast was their biggest since the 'doomsday bomb' tests of 1961-62'"*

The sounds that we do not hear are the sounds of the Mysterious Theatre. The more primitive people hear the spirit world. They know that it is there. The sounds that we do not hear: the wail of the oppressed (if we heard it we could not sleep), the bomb (we would abolish the state), the starving moan the black cracked parched throat (we would abolish money), the monotonous groan of life slipping away while we let go of our lives in useless labor to support a loveless system. No. Wrong. I am wrong. It isn't enough just to hear the sound of the bullet entering the body, thuck, in order to let go of the gun, you have to tune in to the sound which can only be heard after Kundalini rises high among the Chakras. What sound is this? Om? The sound of the voice after the Revolution? With theatrical means this sound can be invoked.

Daily life centers the ear on what is immediately physically audible. Theatre, ritual, trance, alter this. You go past the daily sound barrier.

The theatre has to create sound that opens the ear to the nature of things—to their order—to the terrible and the beautiful, to the mute sound of the exploited sucked out moan and moon, to the great orbs turning in space, the creaking of the ship we're on, to the drone of the slave society, and to the sound of the human spirit after the Revolution, the sound of the whole world eating, the little planet turning in peace.

Rio de Janeiro. 16 October 1970.

* On November 6, 1971, The Atomic Energy Commission exploded a 5 megaton nuclear device on Amchitka Island, the Aleutians.

101

Letter on Women's Liberation. (Judith Malina to Carl Einhorn.)

Croissy-sur-Seine
April 9, 1970

Dear Comrade/Lover/Friend:
      Just got up, untangled Isha's baby arm from around my neck, as she said Mama in her sleep & sat down by the fire before anyone's awake to write you.
      Let me get to the heart of the matter—I have been thinking, reading, talking on the matter of the "position" of women a great deal. Try to remember that we are not typical—in working for the great social revolution of the left, the revolutionary is constantly trying to struggle *towards* and *for* those who are typical. In the Sexual Revolution & in the Liberation of Women no one is typical. You are not typical and I am not typical. What matters is only that you are the slave to your

183

programmed situation like any boss, soldier, cop; just as I am the slave of my programmed female situation like any peasant, wage-worker, black man ... (or soldier or cop) but we are also concerned for the masses of men who enslave their wives & girlfriends in the typical ways: *Kinder-Küche-Kunt*. And what we do and learn affects them: to get to the heart of the matter: the really radical women's position must be that it is far better to relinquish sexual relationships than to allow them to continue under sexist conditions! This is neither more nor less radical than asking a worker to strike (not to work, to render his services, or to enjoy the benefits of work whether material or spiritual) until that worker can work in conditions befitting a human being. However, in terms of the upbringing of children, in terms of social economics the problem is special. It is *not* special psychologically! That's the big lie! The Dumb Bunnies say, "But women need men," or, "But I love men" & so they do (me, too)—and that's no argument against insisting that our needs and our love be fulfilled without degradation & social injustice.

It is important that this not be simplified only to a statement like "I won't sleep with you unless you treat me well" because that's still a form of trade and subservience—though in many cases such things must be said & have been said & are being said now and will be said more —. It must become a strong political position: not alone a position for personal gain. Have you dug Bobby Seale's discussion of women in his interview in *The Movement*? I read a quote in the *Great Speckled Bird*—and he is right on! He says "the overall oppression that exists of different people is not going to be solved without the liberation of women"—and that's from the Black Panther's mouth.

I am standing in the water-sogged boots of every farmer's wife, or the fancy shoes of every 9 to 5 secretary—they are my sisters & we have found each other—and the young women who are used as sex-objects are also my sisters; and the slave who says I love my job, I love my master, is all the more enslaved for the numbing of the heart.

In *The Sexual Revolution* Reich shows how no one can be sexually free in the repressive society and he was somewhat pessimistic in that gray period before our Movement gave hope. But now we are out to change all that—and ("But what can I do?") we must act on this principle: Till the Revolutionary Situation emerges we are all involved in the Old Structure. We understand this economically when we use the slogan "No one is free till all of us are free." We must act on this principle: no one is sexually untainted while the sexual repression continues. Two people can't create a little Eden in the Midst of Hell.

Though we try, God knows we try!

But those of us who have glimmers of love, glimmers of happiness, must not be corrupted by them into believing that we've done more than feed our greed. At best, we've only made it possible "to live on a little" and do our work.

I have always loathed men who misuse women.

Total revolution means no more fucking sexists!

When you—and all your kind—realize first that you *are* the exploiters and second that this power *will* be taken from you whether you fight to defend your male supremacy or not!:

Then we shall work together—eye to eye & hand in hand—and no one shall rule—neither shall men rule women, nor the rich misuse the poor, nor the strong overwhelm the weak, nor the aggressive intimidate the timid.

But none of these things can come about till some of us bring a realistic hopeful tone to that part of the revolution that is concerned with the breaking up of the old order —

No, wishy-washy peacemakers won't do it —

Nor will throwing stones at police at theatrically burning barricades

Nor will battles in which there are even bigger game —

This was a hard page to write. I love you. And I am coming to free the slaves! FREE OUR SISTERS! Free me!

Continued

April 10, 70.

For Lenin's birthday, I read Lenin and Krupskaya. Krupskaya's Memoir of Lenin—and she is a zap of a woman, bold, strong, inspiring all around her. Why do they fill me with hope, when we all know what happened? And Mao too, seriously for the first time—if it weren't for the obsession with the military.

I am sending you in a package copy of an interesting supplement to *L'Idiot Internationale* which Jean-Jacques (Lebel) and other Anarchs made up in collaboration with the Maoists. It was a first attempt to work together & J-J described with great intensity the agony of this attempt—"It was nerve-wracking. It was, in fact, almost *sexually* nerve-wracking to work with people we were in conflict with on that level." What a fine insight—"*sexually* nerve-wracking." Think about that.

THEORY:

    I   Suffering *cannot* be turned into energy.
    II   Hate *can* be turned into energy.
    III   Suffering *can* be turned into hate.
    IV   And then: Hate into energy.

Derivation of this theory.

    A.   Fanon's theory of the inevitability of violence by the oppressed.
    B.   Amerikan (rich) white youth's rage as it rejects the role of oppressor.
    C.   My own need to rage at realizing my own role as Woman in a changing situation.

> That is: I would like to make Stage I–"Suffering into Energy" the whole struggle. But I can't. As pacifist I want to see Stage III eliminated altogether–But I don't know how.

> Total rejection of Stages II & III seems to lead to

>   1) Submission (the end of the liberal line), or
>   2) Enormous Despair

Questions:

> Must the inevitable hate (*if* it is inevitable) lead to annihilative feelings: i.e., the difference between the desire to win & the rage to destroy, both implying violence?

> Gautama, Jesus, Mohandas make a theory in which the sufferer becomes the Active Agent & his suffering becomes the Energizing Act. History shows that this Act breaks down somewhere & turns again either to violence or submission.

> At what point does this breakdown occur?

> What are the alternatives?

I am trying to clear a way through the jungle of confusions. But I don't agree that it's "*only* clear in the doing." Though of course that's where the final definitive clarification comes. Sure we need exemplary action (like Paris, Mai '68) even if we must proceed without theory, without maps, even though we *know* the maps will be, must be inaccurate. I appreciate your pointing out to me the distinction between "a body of theory" and "practical plans." You are right.

I'm not waiting for anyone to "make it clear."

Let's work. All of us, like Lenin & Krupskaya, to do something useful with our short lives.

I am working all the time, waking & sleeping, in dreams, in talk, in reading, at films, eating, shitting, teaching Isha.

I'm working at it. I know you are too.

> FUCK ALL SLOGANS
> (except)
> I LOVE YOU

> Judith

102

Meditations on Revolution.

Comrades,

We are factionalized, and the great opposing camp, the common enemy is not. No human being is my enemy. I claim that "till the day I die." But in the system—which has so many working for it—in its thinghood, in its imagery, among its idols and ikons, I see my enemy. Smash the idols, not the people. Abraham.

But those who constitute the dominating power, tho they squabble among themselves—democrats and republicans, conservatives and liberals, socialists and rightists, fascists and Peronists—they are united against us. We are united against them, but we, the radical revolutionaries, appalled by the blunders of Popular Fronts, accept factionalism in our struggle against the great whale, fish of death, we squirm for purity, knowing that purity if it were sufficiently refined like pitchblende into radium, a drop of it would be enough to precipitate the fall of Capital. We want to fight it out now amongst each other, because when we win we want it to be perfect. But it won't be, not now, not then, not after Mammon falls, not after the Messiah comes, it is forever a process of refinement and mixture.

The theatrical critics never tire of pitting us one against the other. They will have but one lion, and we are all beasts. Of equal magnitude. I find fault with Mao's way, but it feeds all the people, and I don't like Stalin's, and I can pick fault with Castro and with Makhno, with Trotsky, with Kropotkin and Bakunin, with everyone: I don't want violence, I don't want hardcore socialism, I don't want a hardening mass culture, I don't want bureaucracy, I don't want ideological imperialism, but most of all I don't want anymore police state, comrades, most of all I don't want the demon Kapital over us with its inhuman exploitation pushing us towards death, most of all I want an end to racist torture.

I am with the people who sell their labor, their bodies, their lives, to escape starvation in their struggle for life. I am thinking of the women who have to carry water on their heads up the high hills of Rio so that someone can turn on the tap in California, I am thinking of the children who are starving in India so the professors in Kansas can talk about liberty, I am thinking of the unbalanced world, the polluted planet, the imminent apocalyptic disaster when, madness, the world falls down, and the light goes out, and we drown down, too soon.

This is a call for the unification of our forces to bring down the structure. In the creative disorder that ensues we will find our way again. We are unified, remember, by our common utopian dream.

Rio de Janeiro. 1 November 1970.

The revolution is going on now, make no mistake of it, and we can see it now, and we are living it and we announce the acts to each other.

The performers are coming to that point of awareness at which they no longer see themselves as parts of a process over which they have no control. They see themselves not as performers in personal dramas about personal losses, gains, tragedies and triumphs. They see themselves as performers with consciousness of planetary dimension.

We have changed the play. We have already changed it.

We create it as we act it, it's long, it's Epic Theatre.

São Paulo, Brazil. 20 August 1970.

Organization and spontaneity. On the preparation of the mass.

The mass: will be frightened, will hesitate, will hold on to the past, to compulsions, to perverse love.

But they have to know what to expect, so that when it happens—when they make it happen—they will not be bewildered, will know what has to be done, will have a field of reference with which to combat the counter revolutionary propaganda, and some experience, at least in the imagination—in order to project their work, their massive role. All this is necessary input for eventual spontaneous action.

Shears to cut the chains that inhibit action. The shears are the ideas that have never been withheld. That is the work of the theatre, as information medium.

The other half of the work: the organization of the revolutionary vanguard, of those inspiring and courageous workers, those yearning and enflamed ragged masses, holy, ferocious, sweet, along with those fools and heroes, saints, lovers, adventurers, poets, technicians, intellectuals, athletes, students, madmen, beauties, who are going to seize the means of production. The groups of 5 to 50 which first seize control of the factories and show their fellow workers: This is what's happening! This is what you can do! The groups which take over the radio and TV stations and announce: The revolution is on! The groups which lead in taking over the water system and the electricity, the roads, and the food supplies. Who do this in order to distribute goods and services without the money hangups.

That is another kind of theatre. That preparation. Less public. The rehearsals are all closed. No spectators until it happens.

Ouro Preto, Brazil. 27 November 1970.

The revolution cannot be the re-assemblage of the old structure with a new cast of characters, the roles remaining what they were. We do not want to have a new king, but to be a people with holiness in our midst.

Detroit. 12 December 1968.

I don't think Socialism is an essential intermediate step. I think Socialism is revisionist. William Shari. Hancock, New York. April 1970.

When we talk about revolution we are talking about the only thing valid to talk about in our age. Other ages have had other fulcrums. Ours is change.

Contradictions: It is clear that this change has many aspects and that the right of free food comes before the right of free speech, that morality comes after eating (Brecht). That is, the Total Revolution consists of many revolutions, and feeding all the people and stopping all the killing are only the first of many changes to come, the free food and free speech may be dependent on each other; slaves are fed because they work.

Rio de Janeiro. 16 October 1970.

That the frenzy not be frittered away. The problem is that the women themselves move so easily, unconsciously, into the dragnet of recuperation (containment), even as they move unconsciously into what is perhaps the most profound area of the revolution itself. As it has always

190

been since the whole planet moved into the cycle of patriarchal hegemony. The patriarchs, in their revolt against the matriarchs, in their ultimate fearsome annihilation of half of the creature power of the species, in their sadistic relegation of women to an inferior position, classify as a joke every creative female impulse to liberate the receptive beauty of women. When the woman speaks up, and beyond that, acts, it's a joke, and the whole vicious masculine paternalistic musclebound brain reduces the female slave to an image of comic strip gestures. The movement for women's liberation touches the most crucial physical center of the revolution of our era.

I know because I am part woman.

What the women are saying is that the contract of love is no longer valid.

The penis is a bludgeon. That's how it is used. Fucking, the characteristic physical form of love, is a process of pain, domination and submission, of strength and weakness, of pride and humiliation, of master and slave.

What we are is not what we are destined to be. What we do is not what we are destined to do forever. The pattern of our behavior is not fate and is not fatal.

The Social Contract, Master and Slave, whether in the capitalist nations or in the socialist nations is an extension of the Sexual Contract. That is why in the new socialist countries the working class continues to slave, because we comprehend all of life, and extend it, in terms of, and starting from, our comprehension of the Sexual Contract.

The contract (drawn up by a patriarchal society) is based on domination and submission, the man dominates the woman, this is the matrix of the contract, and out of it all human relationships get conceived in terms of domination and submission, of ownership and property, of capital and labor, the sexual form of behavior comes to function as the model for all of our behavior. So that the working person, for example, understanding life in terms of domination and submission, submits economically, and allows the boss to dominate socially, at the same time, of course, that the boss is actively trying to dominate and maintain control (because it feels 'good'). But the complicity of the slaves in this regard must be exposed or we may die like slaves, as we have done for thousands of years.

But, alas, workers of the world, the chains will not disintegrate by wishing it, never. Not until the slaves, the women, rise up and disarm the masters.

The Movement for Women's Liberation focuses on the source of our sickness.

What do our dreams tell us, and anthropological research? That it all began, the myth, in a Golden Age, when as tribes we lived together in balance and harmony, nourished and led by the fertility of women, protected and guided by the strength of men. Then came agriculture, the grain, and with it matriarchy, a communal society replete with virtue and productivity; but the elevation of one sex over another led to sickness, and the worshipped Woman, the Goddess, came to be cruel: corrupted by the very power her brothers and sisters had commended into her person in loving trust, she learned fear: fear that she might fail in her responsibilities, and fear compounded itself and clouded reality, and she confused her fear of inadequacy with fear of loss of power. Power. And she confused the power invested in her, entrusted to her, with the power that flooded her inner being during the act of love, and her lovers were subjected yearly to sacrifice, and the men were made slaves, and eventually the slaves revolted and ran away and became hunters, and then the agriculture was conquered by the hunters, and patriarchy came. And more corruption.

Abel is the hunter. Cain is the agriculture. And God the Father—who is a hunter of souls (de la Vega)—prefers the sacrifice of Abel (the dead meat), and rejects the sacrifice of Cain (the grain) because He had no respect for it, and Cain revolts and kills, and becomes the killer and the hunted and the hunter, and the patriarch Father-God reigns secure, and his priests justify it all. He gives Cain, now that he is also a hunter—having killed Abel—His blessing, His X mark on the forehead, that he be protected, that no one harm him, because he is beloved, he the killer, the beloved killer-hunter of God.

The next development in man. The new heuristic principle. Lancelot Lawes White. Heuristic: means of learning, means of thinking.

There is a recipe for physical love that is not to be found in the *Kama Sutra* nor in the *Arabian Love Manual* but which has been described by disciples of Tantra Yoga. You both get high. High on spirit, on universe, on contemplation of the body, high on sense perception, touching, seeing, tasting, hearing, high on Ganges, on music, incense, odors, immortal longings, high on time, high on each other. Explore the world, explore the world of the body, explore its geography. Each touch a trip beyond the secret isles, beyond the waters of the moon, beyond the bay of flesh, the lake of desire. How long it takes, time stretches, how it glides. The male sits like a lotus, the woman, yoni, engulfs the lingam as she slides around it, like night around the earth, curling her legs in embrace around male hips, arms envelop like vines, like rays of stars, endless bodies, time holds its breath and breathes, it is the sea, the mountain. Mind penetrates mind, the infinite curving in on itself, she holds the universe in her arms, it is he, he holds the cosmos in his arms, it is she. They charge each other with supra life, stoned, vibration, sound, ecstasy, orgasm. Without lingam ever striking yoni, neither aggression nor passivity, nor pain inflicted nor pain received, physical and spiritual union, transcendence, new world, floating, infinite, beyond pleasure: joy. The Hindustani word: *Maithuna:* Union.

When the masochist (I know all about that, because it is my name, my nature and pattern) reaches that moment of sensation at which the parallel between his sexual habits and daily patterns of behavior become objectified, then the changes will begin. When the super-ego comprehends thru feeling that it is acting and suffering according to the pattern fashioned around the libido, then the changes will begin. When the super-ego flashes out on the fact that it is abusing itself, and submitting to psychological pain, cultural deprivation, economic enslavement, political humiliation, and social imprisonment, all because it is accepting without question the basic patterns of apparently normal action, then the changes will begin. We understand the world thru our understanding of our sexual habits; when the super-ego (smart, bright, super intelligent) rebels against this, the super-ego will look for a way out; and the basic pattern, which even communist-oriented revolutions cannot escape, will experience such tremors that the steel portals crack. End of that primal split: Sado/Masochism. So that we no longer play roles, the Master-Sadist and the Masochist-Slave: symbolic images and marks are rent and reality appears and we appear: real to one another, in real relationship to each other: I and Thou.

"We want the Socialist revolution with human nature as it is now: human nature itself cannot do without subordination, without control, without managers and clerks ... We are not Utopians, we do not indulge in 'dreams' of how best to do away *immediately* with all management, with all subordination. These are anarchist dreams based on want

193

of understanding of the tasks of a proletarian dictatorship. They are foreign in their essence to Marxism, and as a matter of fact, they serve but to put off the Socialist revolution until human nature is different." Lenin. *State and Revolution.*

The Socialist revolution of which great Lenin speaks is dependent on a contradiction: the continuation of an intolerable psycho-sexual condition: one of suffering, of "subordination . . . control . . . managers . . . clerks . . ."

The fundamental revolution of culture is the liberation of the sexual pattern: the work of freeing ourselves from our enslavement to our masochistic-sadistic character.

This is not "dreaming," this is not "Utopian": this is fundamental human need: to be free of agony, to be free of a psycho-sexual mentality that constantly gives birth to systems of slavery.

It is an illusion, comrades, and brother Vladimir Ilyich, that the revolution can succeed otherwise: illusion is counter-revolutionary. Neither socialism, nor communism, nor anarchism will ever be anything but sad travesties of their intentions until we effect this change.

Rio de Janeiro. 10 November 1970. Detention Cells. D.O.P.S.
(Department of Political and Social Order).
Belo Horizonte, Brazil. 27 July 1971.

The sexual revolution is the proletarian revolution. Murray Bookchin.

The freeing of the slaves thru the transformation of the unbalanced slave mentality into a mentality of balance: the revolutionary equality we have been talking about for hundreds of years: from insanity to sanity: the escape of the slaves: with it comes escape from the state (the master), the law (the lash), money (the idol before whom we must grovel), property (the burden we must carry), war-police-weapons-jail-violence (the pain to which we submit).

A study of sado-masochist literature, de Sade, Sacher-Masoch, Pauline Réage, Apollinaire, R. Crumb: the sado-masochist rite always leads to the death of the masochist. The escape of the slave may mark the beginning of the escape from death which, in the sado-masochist rite, is the inevitable conclusion. Watch out.

Iowa City (Iowa), U.S.A. 22 January 1969. Detention Cells. D.O.P.S. (Departamento de Ordem Politica e Social). Belo Horizonte, Brazil. 23 July 1971.

103

Meditations on Violence.

OM SRI MAITREYA

Violence is the central theme of the theatre of our time. For the first time in history the authority of violence is being contested in every corner of the world, in every chamber of the mind.

OM SRI MAITREYA

"Let me say at the risk of seeming ridiculous that the true revolutionary is always guided by great feelings of love." Che Guevara.

OM SRI MAITREYA

Only an alternative that is more effective than violence can achieve what the revolution is really all about.

OM SRI MAITREYA

Guns are the Golden Calf of the revolution.

OM SRI MAITREYA

Violent action, violent revolution, changes things, but people remain what they are.

OM SRI MAITREYA

"What do the masses feel about violence? Experience shows that they are pacifistic and afraid of violence. The second question is: What is the relationship between the use of violence (which we know to be necessary) and the masses' attitude towards it? The answer to both questions is, and can only be, the same. *The larger the mass base of the revolutionary movement, the less violence will be required,* and the more also will the masses lose their fear of revolution." Wilhelm Reich, *What is Class Consciousness?*

OM SRI MAITREYA

Armed struggle must not be confused with the revolution. JM.

OM SRI MAITREYA

Class struggle and class war. Struggle does not automatically and inevitably mean war.

OM SRI MAITREYA

"All use of force demoralizes its user." Dühring. "A parson's mode of thinking." Lenin.

But Lenin's put-down does not invalidate the weight of what may be the only thing that Dühring ever said which stands up before the winds.

OM SRI MAITREYA

Violent revolution means power to the party. Nonviolent revolution means power to the people. William Shari.

OM SRI MAITREYA

Nobody is free as long as there are police. There is no communism as long as there are police, because there is no community wherever there are police.

OM SRI MAITREYA

As soon as you get hip to the implications of total revolution, it becomes clear that all the partial revolutions are unacceptable to the degree that they set up barriers to their own objectives.

OM SRI MAITREYA

Man cannot accept the principles of violence or authority in the long run. The person who endorses violence is fractured. Schizophrenia. And the problem for the pro-violent revolutionary is that the people naturally find violence alien, repellent. They may dream of raping and ripping the white mistress, of burning down the mansion, of shooting the bosses and the generals. But they also dream of becoming the master, of behaving like him and of possessing, in vast quantity, chandeliers and women and lackeys, like the master does. What does this prove. That dreams are not unaffected by the corruptive agents of the system. One could also say that every afternoon at four he dreams of love and of another life.

OM SRI MAITREYA

The First Tempter
(a former pacifist)

Feed all the people, if necessary kill the rich, kill the top brass, kill the lousy military anyway, kill the fucking stock brokers, capital punishment, they robbed it all from the poor the working class, kill the flunkeys who protect the rich, kill the police, get them dead and out of the way, over, get it done, but feed the people, the kids, the starving barefoot suffering oppressed.

OM SRI MAITREYA

The Second Tempter
(a radical mystic)

All is one. The seed must die. Not to kill the killer is to kill. Not to kill the germ is to kill the child. The child is pure. The people are children. Not to kill the killer is impure. To kill is to bring forth life.

OM SRI MAITREYA

Winterdale R.D.
Hancock, N.Y.
Mid-April, 1970

Dear Julian,

... Here is an opinion, better, a collection of thoughts, on our mutual problem which, expressed in my different language (nothing really new), may suggest a different tactic ... The truth is that when you are worried I am worried and when you are unhappy I am unhappy and relevant or irrelevant here's my 2¢ worth.

Anarchism and nonviolence are not means or ends of one to the other but synonyms of one another. They are not tactics or strategies but a life style, the revolutionary goal of which, after it has been reached, can be considered the future of humanity. Violence is the State. The State is violence. To consider a violent revolution is like considering an interim State. Neither will wither away.

But what about our unconvinced comrades? Isolating ourselves from them is no answer. Hermits are full of shit. The Work of the World is in the world. And our comrades are out there working. Our place is with them, demonstrating with our minds and our bodies, the strength and clarity of our work with them, that our lives are THE lives, our actions the correct action. To work with them is not to say that we must go out and blow up police stations or learn karate but create in, around and through them correct alternate actions; we must act strongly and fearlessly, propagandize them, but with the Propaganda of the Deed; we must act forcefully and in concert with our brothers.

Now *of course* feeding the people is prime and *of course* a socialist 'revolution' will feed more people (for a while at least) but these 'revolutions' are reform movements (I almost said *only* reform movements, but how can any relief be invalid to a starving man? Chairman Mao's and Chairman Nixon's food both fill stomachs.) And it is important that our brothers recognize them for what they are. (Would guerrilla distribution, for example, be less efficacious?) We must charge into the alternative, live in the alternative society, deal with our sisters and brothers as though they share our ideals. They will. They do. They need only the courage of our example.

They need to be re-educated away from the tragic and death oriented notion that nonviolence is a tactic, which has been cynically foisted on them by the philistines. The Anarchist Society is the strategic goal. The Work is the tactic. Non-violence is the life-style, the life-form, the non-death from which the weapons of revolution are formed.

Life-faith is the semen which fertilizes the egg of discontent, is the warm ambience in which it matures into the revolutionary act, the nutriment which allows it to grow into The Permanent Revolution. Violence is death, white bread, the burning cold, the ultimate chromosome deranger. Non-violence is no philosophic notion, no clever tactic/weapon against which the Great Opposing Camp is sometimes unable to raise a defense. It *IS* the life-force, the creative source.

There is no need for us to fear for our 'ideals' or be careful of our 'behavior' in the 'violent situation.' We will act. We will criticize later. Our actions will be as correct as our faith in life, as strong as our creative energy, as effective as our contact with reality. Our criticisms do not inhibit us, they construct. They instruct and inspire us to further delight, further action. They are the musical accompaniment to our Dance of the Revolution and dancing is the ground simulation of flying.

Our wish is our watchword, and the only one for these times,

Love and Peace in the Revolution

Bill (Shari)

OM SRI MAITREYA

And what of violence to property?

The trouble with violence to property is that people see in it justification for violence done to human beings. It evokes fear. It provokes violence in the defense of property.

What is the use of violence to property? Symbolic efficacy? Beyond that one might, for instance, destroy weapons, burn money, police records . . .

How can we define the circumstances then under which violence to property is non-destructive to life and the life-spirit. And might it not be a better way to express violent rage than by acting violently towards people?

Is the suggestion that all violence—to both property and life—is bad the phony ethics of a violent ruling class which respects property more than life? Which shoots at thieves?

Crossing the river into reason.

199

OM SRI MAITREYA

I am anti-violent out of recognition of my own violent nature.

I am anti-violent because I see too the violence of the structure, of the enemy, of the theatre, of my comrades.

I am anti-violent because I see that the violence which we have not yet abnegated has brought us to the point at which our society is based on fear. And the dangers of this widespread fear are so great (they could in the end be fatal) that steps must be taken immediately against them. The fear is rooted in the violence which we admit, permit, excuse and empower.

OM SRI MAITREYA

faced by the spread of wars of national liberation
the cult of armed violence offensive and defensive
the iconography of the heroic guerrilla

faced by the guilt in the loins engendered by imperialism and
        capitalist cream
faced by the success of the armed strategies of the f l n in algeria
of castro and guevara and the n l f in vietnam
and of china
the pacifist anarchist must analyze wars of liberation
and alternatives

and must
create
a logical nonviolent strategy

which gives hope
for the destruction of imperialism

OM SRI MAITREYA

If anybody asks me what I think about violence, says Judith, I would say that (I think it's inevitable BUT that) I am working to diminish its dictatorial grip on action and history; I consider my work the effort to loosen that grip.

200

OM SRI MAITREYA

Rudi Dutschke. 7 March 1968:

"The Revolution is not an event that takes two or three days, in which there is shooting and hanging. It is a long drawn out process in which new people are created, capable of renovating society so that the revolution does not replace one elite with another, but so that the revolution creates a new anti-authoritarian structure with anti-authoritarian people who in their turn re-organize the society so that it becomes a non-alienated human society, free from war, hunger, and exploitation."

OM SRI MAITREYA

The key to the exorcism of violence is the sexual revolution.

OM SRI MAITREYA

There will be violence in the revolution. How could it be otherwise? We cannot postpone the revolution till violence is purged from the earth. But in the course of the revolution violence is going to give way utterly to the force of love (*Ahimsa*), probably around the same time that the sexual revolution completes the first phase of its operation with the exorcism of body guilt and with the release of some of the terrible points of pressure caused by sexual fear and frustration. Therefore we start with the children now.

OM SRI MAITREYA

blessed are thou o lord our god
who hast created evil
that we may devise against it

OM SRI MAITREYA

Hail to the Buddha to come!

OM SRI MAITREYA

he is the peace
that exists only in the people
unified

OM SRI MAITREYA

104

Project: A Film: HOW TO REVOLT:

> The use of film or video for conveying information about the revolution. With compendium of nonviolent strategies. To be shown on walls, in the street, in social halls, apartments, cellars, wherever people can gather. But until this film is played out in life ... and until we have at our disposal nonviolent techniques for accomplishing these changes, revolutionary change depends on violent solutions, and will suffer the inevitable corruption that must follow violent revolution. Therefore we speak of the need, inevitably, or nonviolent revolution.

San Francisco. 18 November 1971.

105

Meditation on Anarchy.

Anarchy is order. Government is civil war. Anselme Bellegarrigue. 1848.

Anarchism is organization, more organization, and still more organization. Alexander Berkman. 1928.

I know my mind's unruled or anarchist by its nature so I suppose society should be. Allen Ginsberg. 1970.

anarchism is order unruled
to rule is to coerce
Allen's mind is "unruled" because it is free

coercion is force
does not free
is violence

anarchism
is
not violence

free organization is harmony
the harmony of anarchy is the harmony to which we are unaccustomed
the state is always coercive

organization is cooperation
cooperation is free
and knows not coercion

cooperation is organization is harmony is anarchy
harmony is not chaos is cooperation
and is free

anarchy is harmony
is not chaos
is free

anarchy is not coercion
is not violence
is organized

and free

106

The great thing is to end in beauty. (Genet.)

How then to create the Great Beauty Play, and that beauty which has not been seen?

Because beauty as we know it and experience it is not enough.

And because ethics (the right hand of the body of which beauty is the breast) are a withered limb they way they have been shaped by authoritarian regimes and capital.

That is why we need to create another aesthetic.

What is it then, this new beauty?

It is something, rainbow-like, which renders the look of life free of blight, star-like above the stars, which touches the heart so that it changes its beat and arouses desire which unlocks the strength which we must unlock in order to do what must be done.

Grenoble, France. 5 May 1969.

The Great Beauty Play:

To drench people with such beauty
that we all will want to crash out of the ugliness,
destroy it and convert its energy into life.

To drench people in such beauty
that it will urge us all out of the morass of misery which is
              civilization,
drawing us all irresistibly, magnetically,
with the great attractive pull of beauty we have never known,
whose acquaintance we have all been denied.

Granville (Ohio), U.S.A. 5 December 1968.

107

The Great Beauty Play:

It is the demonstration of the efficacy and efficiency
       of counter-violent revolutionary action
         thru a successful nonviolent campaign.

That is, we can talk in great gorgeous
            high flying wide wingspread words
            about action without violence,
but the talk will remain rhetoric
            and romantic,
            until we prove that it works:

            Find a way.
            Make it work. Jackson MacLow.

We must move from theory
            into action.
This will last longer than five hours:
            maybe ten years or more

This epic which we have to enact:
            To find the strategy:
            To plan the campaign:
            To gather together

            the large cast of characters:
            all the good anarchist pacifist performers:
            and go to it.

            Until consummation.

If the revolution
            as we understand it today
            is going to take 30 to 50 years:

then the first stage
            should be accomplished within the
            next 10-15 years.

This play takes place in reality:
            We have to take over
            an area somewhere:

and create
            ENCLAVE 1
            a free anarchic non-coercive community
                        of several hundred thousand people or more.

And we have to do this in such a way that:
> all the soldiers resign,
> all the doors open,
> all the guns go blind
> all the people eat and all
> the killing stops.

That's the scenario
> for the only play
> i am interested in doing.

The international counter-revolution will follow.
> The international counter-revolution will probably defeat
> ENCLAVE 1

But we will have found
> the techniques:
> the legs to carry us on.

Bar-sur-Aube, France. 28 April 1969.

108

Meditation on Self Defense. Questions. 1971.

First we have to be sure it is self defense and not aggression in the guise of self defense.

Then we must not use an exceptional instance as if it were the norm: the maniac is about to kill the baby, what do you do? Well, you try to live your life in such a way that at that decisive moment you make a good choice—(what is a *good* choice? or a *right* choice?)—; or, you try to overpower the maniac without killing; or, given the choice between killing the maniac (who is the maniac?) and letting the maniac kill the baby, either you do nothing, or you kill the maniac. But you do not let this exceptional incident become the excuse for the general use of violent attack and retaliative modes of behavior.

Then what is throwing a bomb? And is it self defense, considering that the established powers are killing us?

Terrorism as self defense?

The hesitation is *embourgeoisement?* Bourgeois moral corruption?

Creative action is ending, or trying to end, the cycle of violence, the luxury of those who eat?

Are we responsible to what we think?

Or is it questionable whether or not we are responsible to our bourgeois (exploitive) thoughts and souls? If those thoughts and souls be bought with privilege *and* force of arms?

First feed all the people, *then* stop all the killing?

If by killing a few thousand, or a few million, or ten or twenty million, you could feed billions . . .?

A recognition of military power in the hands of capital as the equivalent of being menaced by a maniac?

The yoke of violence begins with economic deprivation or with sexual frustration or with the principle of self defense?

It is easy (easier?) to abandon the principle of self defense when there is no enemy, and only then?

When do we defend ourselves against ourselves, against our sexual frustration, against the moral principles of our violent scene? When do we get out from under?

It is better to die than to kill?

What does better mean in that sentence?

Never to kill?

Is this the abstract philosophizing that is upper class consciousness? Are philosophy, morals, holiness-in-abstraction, are these the conditioned thought of privilege which does not take into account the holy (life) necessities of those whom society has condemned to physical suffering?

Morally, may people who are starving kill for bread, or for bread for their perishing children? Never to kill? Shall we tell them this? Shall we say, *Ahimsa*, Love Force, truth, holiness, life is sacred, die, but do not kill?

Gandhi says that the *Satyagraha*—the warrior armed with truth and love—must, like any soldier, be ready to die, but, unlike any soldier, he refuses to kill: he must be yet more courageous . . .

What is self defense for the starving?

Can the revolutionaries—who manage to eat—I mean the intellectuals who largely fill the ranks of the revolutionaries today—take it upon themselves to kill "in self defense" *for the starving* if, for example, the starving are too weak, apathetic, too unaware, unorganized, etc., to act (violently) in their own defense?

In the face of this reasoning, can the anarchist pacifist say, "End the tactics of violence!"?

The anarchist pacifist can say, "End the tactics of violence," *only* if his work provides a plan of action to alleviate the suffering of the starving, of the masses, *immediately?*

If we fail to do this . . . the consequences . . . of history . . .

If we fail to do this we must use violence.

If we use violence, do we risk increasing the spiral of violence until the whole human race dies, the starving man?

OK?

Everyone?

Maybe?

OK?

In self defense of the planet, of the man, of the starving children, an end to violence, murder, absolutely?

The circle thus closes on violence, invalidates, and disarms it.

Is there another choice, but life?

San Francisco. 20 November 1971.

109

The theatre is the Wooden Horse by which we can take the town.

Paris. 30 October 1967.

110

from 2 Conversations on Revolutionary Theory

JM: Isn't it clear. for instance,
        that the students get into anarchism
           because the poetry of anarchism
             rings true for them.
             And they are right.
        But the people who earn their bread
           by the sweat of their brows
           can't grasp the poetry
           because they are always walking
             on unfirm ground,
           and anarchism and its poetry
             look too risky.
    They don't know how they'd make out out there.
    They need the poetry of practicality.
    Someone needs to do this for them.
        in a way that does not make this someone
        into a leader.

Except that we are conditioned
    to follow the leader.

JB: A society based on insecurity
    is going to create a
    psychologically insecure
    people looking for someone to lean on.

JM: Maybe
        a group of people
          a cell,
              or what used to be called
              a congress
      could create this clarity.

    Of course
        the anarchists shy away from such a project
        because they want to leave open
        as much space as possible
          for spontaneity

    The people
        will be spontaneous
        when they are not afraid of the great void,
        when, like actors improvising,
          they are clear about the objective.

JB: This is what our research has taught us:
        when we played free theatre in *Paradise Now*
        we were freest
        when the objective was clearest

        and that when we reached the objective
        there was still ample space and time
          for the spontaneous,
          the unforeseen.

Lenin, citing Karl Kautsky:
        " 'Modern Socialist consciousness can rise
    only on the basis of profound scientific knowledge.
    The vehicles of science are not the proletariat
        but the *bourgeois intelligentsia*.

It was out of the heads of members of this stratum
that modern Socialism originated,
    and it was they
    who communicated it
        to the more intellectually developed
                        proletarians
    who in their turn,
        introduce it into the proletarian
                class struggle . . . ' "

Daniel Guérin:
"The anarchist finds himself,
    just like his brother-enemy the marxist,
    seized by a grave contradiction.
The spontaneity of the masses
    is essential,
        has priority over everything,
        but it is not enough.
In order to reach the consciousness of the mass
the assistance of a revolutionary minority
capable of figuring out the revolution
reveals itself as indispensable.
How to avoid
    this elite capitalizing on its superior
                    intellectuality,
        substituting it in place of the masses,
        paralyzing their initiative,
        indeed, imposing on them
              a new domination?"

Proudhon:
All revolutions
    are accomplished
        by the spontaneity
            of the people . . .
Revolutions
    do not recognize
        initiators:
They happen
    when they are called
        by the signal given them
            by the destined;

```
                they stop
                    when the mysterious force
                        which made them explode
                            is exhausted."

JM:             The inherent contradiction:
                la force mystérieuse
                will not release itself
                until the psychological blocks
                that prevent us
                            from dividing all the food equally
                            are removed,
                and until there is at least a plan
                shedding clear light on how it can be done.



JM:             The next theoretical problem
                which the nonviolent anarchists must face is:
                        the unification of the classes
                            through the destruction of the class system.
                The great problem is to raise our common humanity
                            so that it breaks thru
                            the heavy crusts of class
                            past the hostility
                            into the reality
                            of our human need
                            to love.
```

Paris. 30 March 1970.

111

The theatricalization of life will draw us into a dream drama in which we choose our own roles. The free will which the Creator Spirit left us as he tore his own self free from us (the *Zimzum*) leaves us free to emerge from the dark prison waters.

And when the deep ego rises from the ocean's floor, it emerges a hero, the upward plunge itself heroic: all escape is heroic.

This is the invisible ray. This is why the work of making the revolution into conscious theatre is essential to our strategy: theatre is a dream, and life. Everything has led to this moment, this realization: the realization of the dream.

The subject matter of the dream is always transformation. We will all be playing out the changes. Changing first from the fearful dream of the alienated individual into the dream of unification in which there is no longer a "they" and "it."

Killing: the dream of the ultimate alienating act. Death: the dream of ultimate annihilation (self). Life: the dream of being: ultimate and conscious union (all and everything: One.)

112

There will be no condescension in the art that speaks to the people. The bourgeoisie are flabby because they are conditioned by a flabby way of life: and their flabbiness of mind, spirit, and body expects, wants, condescension from art, from everything.

The theatre of the people never condescends. Condescend to those who hold the keys to our salvation? To those who are the nearest to God? To those who are furthest from corruption? To those who know how to endure? To those who are eventually going to free us all? To those with whom we hope to be One?

113

The impulse to live, for the stone to speak, the ocean, mother of things, to give birth, to walk onto the beach: this impulse survives in everyone's quasi instinctive desire to be an actor or actress, to take the voyage out of the self, out of the meanness of daily life, out of ungratifying existence into true being. Everyone wants to be someone else, or that aspect of himself which is so different that it seems like someone else. This is the basis of revolutionary hope: divine discontent. To be part of what could be. To enact the imaginary, to act, to fulfill the wish. The essence of anarchy: the condition in which each can choose any role in life and act it out.

Ergo: all power to the people.

Cannes to Aix-en-Provence, France. 16 May 1970.

114

after the revolution
there will be wine under the trees
there will be forms of love shaped like the great bear
when i say my love is a native in another country i will be
      telling the truth
i will plunge my head deep into your wine dark cunt the moist
        lips like the lapping of salt water rolling past my ears
        folding back upon my neck and then i'll breathe hard
bread will be scarce and everyone will eat it
when the revolution comes
romance will be finished
but what is begun

after the revolution
when we are all exhausted like lovers

i will openly grope the delicatessen man with all my fingers
you and i will lie limpid and hungry
the problem of food distribution will debilitate the cause
but the scent of liberated loins
and the glorious autumn weather
will keep our cocks erect

when the revolution comes
you will be standing at the prow and the salt wind blows in
          your face
for hundreds of years you dreamt of the ocean
now you are wet

from "Songs of the Revolution":
New York City. 1964.

115

FACTA NON VERBA.

Don't talk; do it.

From this point on the revolutionary rhetoric only serves to fritter
away the frenzy; it becomes an excuse not to act. It is time, perhaps,
1971, for a phase in which we are quieter. Methodical. Clear. Direct.
And active.

116

what actions can we take

1. teach the children the small ones
    infiltrate the educational system
    blow the kids' minds
    prepare them

    form free schools
    give all our knowledge away
    study the revolution and teach it

    widen the spirit
    initiate great dreams

2. infiltrate industry
    talk to the farm laborers the workers the poor
    help them to organize themselves
    to combat their daily misery
    rent medical aid exploitation harrassment
    help them to recognize the reality of their oppression

3. infiltrate the media
    whoever can
    but remember they're geared to speak for the system

4. start communes
    we need to figure out the problems
    like how to supply each other with what we need
    we need also to supply examples of communal solutions
    and of social relations that work

5. found newspapers magazines make posters illegal radio tv
            stations that can transmit and jam the main lines
    with vivid information
    tell the people what the revolution is for what against
    how to do it
    open ears to new sound of whole earth

6. make free stores
    get people habituated
    to the idea of free
    give yourself away

7. infiltrate the army the police

8.   form cells

        groups of five are good
        people you know intimately and can trust
        soon it may not be as easy for us as it is now
        people you can work together with easily
        study a craft
        or an industry we may have to supply our own needs during
                harder times
        study the revolution together
        organize a place for public discussions
        get to know the police of your city
        study medicine
        first aid
        police and military tactics and how to subvert them
        study the jails the architecture
        study the courts
        and oil and science
        study electronics
        and cybernetics

        and publicize the information

        study the city plans
        how to gum them up and make them function like poems

9.   deliver mail free
        find time in your life to do free services
        repair cars
        clean streets
        the digger thing
        it undermines the props of the system
        it blows people's minds
        it makes light enter
        it lifteth the spirit

10.   write on the walls

11.   figure out how to take over the system
        how to distribute the food
        how to produce it
        and all the other stuff we need

and be sure there are enough workers ready and people to
    start living without money without police army state
    and prisons all forms of coercion
and do it

12.   the cell that flashes the people with
        an experience of beauty
so that they have something to move towards
and of the ugliness to move away from
because the sense of beauty is gone
and with it the sense of god goodness and the creative
and what remains is the ugly destruction
that can only be answered by our beauty
therefore
anywhere
just by our being there
the confrontation happens
as we walk down the street and in public places
the love force in the face

remembering always
that we have to re-create beauty and love
because beauty and love as we know them have been shaped by
authoritarian capitalism and loaded with its content

13.   clusters working together
network of affinity groups processing anarchist theory
        and practice

14.   autogestion syndicates
network of workers voluntarily unified processing anarchist
        theory and practice

15.   be more specific

if necessary
develop exercises
to sharpen our thinking

the hard work
of transforming the poetry

into planning
the plans
into action

*Ithaca (New York), Boston, the Atlantic (New York City to
Cherbourg). December 1968 — April 1969. Paris. July 1970.*

16.   keep inventing further actions
        as long as necessary

San Francisco. 5 December 1971.

117

Meditation. New York to Berlin. 1964-1970.

I tremble that all this might someday shatter and fade away: delicate
sphere within which I move so pleasurably sustained: family, community, work, theatre, enough to eat, the privilege of traveling around from
country to country as we play our plays, I ride in a VW bus and
sometimes a hair out of the mane of the horse of temporal Fame
brushes a cheek, outside the moving window and inside the moving
brain, it's like too much of good fortune, and all the time that we ride
around in these buses, all these years, I live in dread that it might one
day just fade away.

But as it becomes evident that the privilege we enjoy is untenable, and
the pleasure and satisfactions of the life we lead illusory, and when all
our studies, our exercises, our performances, encounters, when everything we have learned, and maybe when all the drugs we have taken
awaken us: satori:

life is a dream
he only wakens
who has set the world aside

So we decided we must leave the theatre and all the charms she secretes:

When we parted in Berlin I kept repeating Garga's words from the end of *In the Jungle of Cities:* "It was the best time." And we fell upon each other's necks and wept. Because the best was not enough.

The end is always the beginning, as it is said. The striving for mutation, that is, the vigorous attempt to bring on that change which is really going to propel us into the next development in man. Knowing of course all the time that one cannot very likely precipitate such a change consciously. When the Messiah comes we will all say: Ah, so that's how!

Permanent Revolution! The turning of the wheel! The discovery of the wheel being the mechanical conquest of space, and the turning of the wheel, chakra, in the mind, in the spirit, being the psycho-conscious-mechanical conquest of stagnation.

The summer of 1969: realization, finally, for us, The Living Theatre, that the time has come to enact the change. We have to, and we have lived our lives in such a way that we have no other choice. The Living Theatre, as institution (which was its fate, living life as it has lived it), The Living Theatre as projection of anarchist community (which it is only in process of becoming) has to transmute. 1969: the decision to dissolve and re-form, as cells, to meet our own needs and the needs of the time.

It is on board the *Cristoforo Colombo* en route from Málaga to Palermo that the *prise-de-conscience* occurs. After two months secluded in Morocco working on a new play which we alternately called *The City Absolute, Saturation City,* and *Penetration City.*

The work: good, tho laborious.

The plan of the play: To go to a city, a town, a village: to stay there anywhere from two to six weeks depending on the size of the place: to do plays all over, in the streets, in markets, plazas, in factories, supermarkets, department stores, in front of public buildings, police stations, buses, subways, at airway terminals, schoolyards, store windows, in parks, on roofs, in courtyards, backyards, in tents, corridors, alleys, empty lots. To change the vibrations of the city. To flash out consciousness on the street. To accustom people to action, to begin by leading people into action within the plays . . .

September 1969: Not unhappy with the work, nor with each other, but we know that neither the ideas for *The City Absolute* nor their execution can be realized if we don't change ourselves. The Living Theatre has become an institution, some thirty four adults and nine children: an impractical situation. Institutions are made by success and our success made us dependent on the income we received from being an institution. Dependent on the money from paid admissions in large theatres. By making us successful, the society has made us dependent on its system. Everything that we learned during the years of our gorgeous exile together, wandering from city to city doing plays, gypsy caravan, time honored strolling players, everything that we learned from the *Paradise Now* trip, brought us to this moment. In *Paradise Now* had we not brought the audience to the doors of the theatre and said, "The Theatre Is In The Street!"? And, did we not stand there, at the doors, face to face with the police? The police, who do not allow theatre in the street, who do not want life to reach and surpass the privileged position occupied by art, who do not want the streets to be free. It was there, at the doors of The Theatres, that we knew that the street was where we had to go.

To do this new play, to go out in the streets, we need a special strength. The old Living Theatre's form can not give strength for this kind of art and work. The old Living Theatre had been formed to do another kind of work and something in its nature would prevent us from taking the necessary measures. That much was clear.

Nevertheless while we inhabited our old shell as a community it has been possible for us to conceive of *The City Absolute*, of a form for playing the streets. In the same way, it is possible for our present society to conceive of life without the constraints of capitalism and bureaucracy. Possible to conceive but impossible to realize. It is possible for instance for our society to conceive of peace and never have it because the nature of the form of life we live does not and never will permit it.

118

for judith
with the hope that we shall one day see together the beautiful
nonviolent anarchist revolution

119

we need
as they
say
to organize

we need
to create
cells

we need
to gather
the forces

we need
to learn
from each other

we need
to give
to each other

i suggest
that we gather
together

all of us
whose work
is the theatre

and study
like lenin
the measures

to be taken
to turn the wheel
of the world

then the cells
like seeds
scatter

and fertilize the world

this is a call
to work out our salvation
together

because i need you
and we are all
in deep need

therefore we must
find a place
find a time

issue the call
find the people
gather

do it

Paris. 15 December 1967.

223

120

Ouro Preto, Brazil. 4 April 1971:

Andrew Nadelson:
Judith, when you were talking about masochism and altriusm you spoke of Erotic Politics and when we were discussing the Social Structure we were concerned with what alternative we offer the people in the street. The way to give the people in the street the knowledge of their power will be by putting ourselves in their power: which is masochistic: their natural response will be sadistic.

Judith:
Exactly. Then the point is: at that moment in the performance to take them and turn them to the erotic, and that's the trick: if we put ourselves in a position in which the people control us, then we are vulnerable, and the traditional response is for them to be sadistic. Now at that moment that they turn sadistic, we have to turn them to an erotic action. The slave who becomes master becomes sadistic and vengeful. The thing is to turn it to the erotic.

Birgit Knabe:
The word erotic bothers me.

Steven Ben Israel:
In the true essence of the word, the erotic is near to God. The neurotic society stifles the erotic and perverts it.

Birgit Knabe:
I think the name Eros is very mixed up on the planet: Wasn't Aphrodite jealous and didn't she punish him?

Judith:
Psyche was the soul—Aphrodite, of course, the Goddess of physical love. Aphrodite, the love goddess, is jealous of the soul, and this is the story of the battle between physical and spiritual love; and Eros, the

erotic element, is used here as the turning point between physical and spiritual love. Eros, the erotic element, is bound in marriage to the soul, and because of the jealously of the love goddess, there is a limitation placed —

Birgit:
But it was placed as a *punishment*—
Psyche not being able to look at Eros—

Judith:
That's a modern interpretation: It is a limitation placed on the body by an Aphrodisian position. In the story, Psyche and Eros could visit each other only at night, but Psyche wanted to see her lover and one night she lit a candle and when she tried to see him in the light she dropped some hot wax on him, he woke and it was all over—because the Greeks could never accept the relation between the erotic and the spiritual. Because they came from a slave society in which the women were oppressed and despised, a society as degenerate as ours. But they saw things in this clear way—they saw that because they were hung up on Aphrodite—who is a Sado/Masochist figure—they saw that Aphrodite was afraid of the soul, afraid of being seen by the soul. Now this civilization is over: because of this. And if we do not find a way to make this light visible—the light in which the erotic and the spiritual come together erotically and spiritually—then we will be over, and we can have only sadistic and masochistic Master/Slave relationships.

Steven Ben Israel:
This is the basis of Wilhelm Reich's *The Murder of Christ.*

Judith:
It is the basis of all of Reich's theory. All communication begins with Eros.

Vicente:
The people, when they become masters, forget that they were once slaves, and if we transform the slaves into masters, then —

Judith:
I am saying that the slave must be transformed without becoming a master. When people find themselves rebelling, at the moment they feel that they can seize the power they can become either a master, or they can change the world and not become a Master but a Great Lover: in

the GREAT sense of the word. And this holy condition: in which one is not a slave nor a master I call erotic. Birgit objects to the word erotic. I would suggest she use the word holy. I prefer the word erotic because it relates especially to the problem of Masochism and Sadism. Conventionally people think of masochism and sadism as erotic forms and they certainly arouse us erotically and everybody has a little of this in them, and some much. But we know that this form of behavior is actually a rejection of real human communication—it's a cut-off of feelings. But in our limitations and neurotic lives, it is sometimes the only feeling we can find. If people beat each other for neurotic reasons, it is because there is a limitation to their erotic condition: Because they can't feel, they arouse feeling by these perversions because it's at last at least some feeling. People who can't feel anything at all or who are afraid to feel can still feel pain. This is the last available feeling. It is the bottom of the range of feeling. If we know that Masochism and Sadism are substitutes for erotic love, are a method of feeling something when you can't feel the real thing, the way to get rid of the Masochism and Sadism, to transcend them: is to discover the real erotic love. This is true socially, culturally, sexually, and politically.

Vicente:
It is easier for the Masochist to come to the Sadist position . . .

Judith:
Sure, because the social structure has it so, it supports the drive from Masochist to Sadist. All the slaves want to be masters. None of the masters want to be slaves. But socially speaking, not sexually. Politically, if we take, for instance, the sadists in Brazil to be the 1% ruling class, if the sadistic class is the ruling class, then it's only 1% of the population. This 1% must change. But nothing is going to make them change because they have all the guns, power, computers. The only thing that will make them change is if the 99% make them change. In this sense I am not a gradualist, but a revolutionist. I do not think that the world will change by making an appeal to the 1%. I think the 99% have a better chance if they refuse to be the slaves and take this sadistic power away. Otherwise, as you say, this 1% will not give up their power because the whole structure supports this hierarchical system. But the people can refuse to be slaves. And because there are so many more of them they can change the whole thing.

Steve Israel:
You really can't say that only 1% of the society is sadistic but that

100% of the society is sadistic: because by the very nature of hustling each other every day we have to be sadistic whether we want to or not.

Judith:
Those who got rich did so because they are the most ruthless. The most cruel.

Steve Israel:
The super-perverted. Yes.

Ivanildo:
But don't the slaves collaborate? Doesn't their condition imply acceptance on their part?

Judith:
I would say this: the organized master/slave relation begins with a power drive which is essentially a sadistic desire and is accompanied by ruthlessness. The cruelest person takes the power and with physical and economic force enslaves another group of people. Nobody wants to be a slave. Clear. Originally the choice is given: slavery or death. To take a Brazilian example: the Blacks submitted to slavery, the Indians chose death. Gilberto Freyre points this out clearly. Now, once having chosen to live as a slave rather than die, which is not a masochistic choice, but a human choice, the question is: how do you live as a slave and survive? Two possibilities: historically: to wait for the revolutionary moment when you liberate yourself or accept the condition. In so far as the position is accepted it is masochistic. In so far as it is used as a ground for rebellion, it is not. At the revolutionary moment—and that can be at any moment—there is no longer a choice between Revolution and Death but between Masochism and Freedom. Right now all the people of the world are beginning to choose against slavery. Our work is to awaken everyone to their revolutionary potential, to show that there is another position that breaks with Masochism, so that the acceptance of slavery is not necessary. Freyre, as fascist pig, admires the masochistic role of the Brazilian slave, and—intelligent master that he is, knowing how to twist the position—says: "Without the slave, Brazil would never have been developed." And since it is a good thing that Brazil developed, he argues, it is good that there were slaves: this is his position, and therefore he endorses the history of slavery in Brazil. Freyre exemplifies the attitude of the intellectual master towards the masochistic slave: "Slavery and Masochism are good." We say both are bad. But until we recognize the masochism as masochism we will not have a

revolutionary situation because people will say: "Of course no one wants to be a slave—Everyone wants to be free—So if people are slaves there must be a reason—because no one would accept it—it must be only the power of the masters . . ."

But a revolt against the Sadism of the masters is insufficient, is not total. The people must revolt also against their own masochistic slavery. When the people see the acceptance of their condition as masochism, they can change it, they can make the revolution.

The revolution:
in the place of the politics of Sadism and Masochism: eroticism, erotic politics.

121

Notes, Plans for Action, Themes for Plays, Pamphlets, Discussions, Material for communication/conversation/ speech/work with the People In the Street, the Worker, the Unemployed.

What to say to the people in the street:
That money is not essential to natural order; that we can live better without it than with it. That we don't need barter either.
That the people need only to produce what is necessary for everyone, and to distribute it without using money.
That the food and materials we need can be brought to open markets and storehouses, and people can come and take what they need.
That in order to produce enough food, clothing, shelter, etc., for everybody in the world everyone needs to work about two months a year.
That the remaining time can be used for leisure, love, creative work, grooving, ecstasy, as each one wishes.
That we can —in association with the people with whom we live and work—decide what our needs are: friendly and efficient units.
That these needs can be processed with the aid of computers, and simple ways can be found to route materials to where they are wanted/needed.

That the working man can manage industry (the factory) himself without orders from 'superiors,' without a managerial class telling him what to do. AUTOGESTION.

That, once we do away with money, we can do away with government, police, armies. End of punitive systems. End of ownership. End of private property means opening of possibility, opening of heart, means whatever you need you can get. Means mutual aid, survival, freedom, life against death.

That we can do without jails. Stealing begins not to exist at the moment at which we abandon private property.

That we don't need mental *institutions* (ill-disguised jails). We can take care of our brothers and sisters without metal and bars.

That it could begin when *the people* take action and refuse to use money anymore, seize the means of production—the factories the fields—and continue to produce, distributing what they produce free and producing *only* what is necessary, no more shit (waste). The difference between shit (waste) and pleasures. Pleasures as necessities. Redefinition of pleasures as desires, desires related to human holy physical wants, not the wants of money, prestige, privilege, power . . .

Make it clear:

That the work force of the world will increase by millions upon millions of people—all those people who are now engaged in superfluous labor: for instance, all the people working in stores selling things, because there will be no more money transactions, no time and labor to be consumed by the process of buying and selling—all these people will be free to do other work. All the people who are doing unnecessary work will stop doing it:

all the people who are working in offices writing things down about money, about how much goes in and comes out, all the people who work in banks, all the construction workers building the banks and the places where this kind of work happens, all the people who mine the iron to make these buildings, who quarry the stone, who bake the bricks, and carry them, who make the paper that they write useless things on, and all the people in the armies, and the police, and the people who manufacture the guns and the tanks and the bombs the list goes on and on millions and millions of people!

All these people, how they are going to be free to do useful things and to rest, to dream, to make love, to create the world.

We don't need to make shoes that wear out so soon because there are already more durable materials and better ways to make things last. We don't need all that advertising and propaganda telling us what to buy and making us greedy for things we don't either want or need; because all we need is a simple announcement telling what's available.

Further INFORMATION
On the Movement: that there is a movement of people all over the planet, in almost every country, seeking to transform the world.

On how we are living in the first phase of a movement of transformation which may take 30 or 50 years to complete itself.

On how this change towards what people truly desire will be made by a combination of study and preparation followed by action.

On how the people must figure it out by themselves, not some leader, but the people who are the ones who know how bad it is, who are suffering, and who are getting to know how good it could be if it were different.

On how we could do this—how we could achieve the objectives of the nonviolent anarchist revolution—if we start now, and work, with lust.

On living in harmony with the earth and with each other.

On the Struggle Period: when the ruling classes say, "No! We must use money!"; and when they come with guns: what can be done to disarm them. On preparatory work within the army, the police, and the minds of the people.

On preparing ourselves to be free, free to think and act. On how our minds are not free in the society within which we now live.

On the relation between sexual liberty and all other liberty.

On preparing ourselves to act without violence. On exorcising the procilivity towards violence, violent responses to stimuli. On ending the cycle of violence.

On bringing up our children permissively so that they get accustomed to freedom and to want more of it. To want more of it than we can yet give them. So that they can go further. On teaching them to love, and to love freedom. In 10 or 15 years the children will be making the movement . . .

On teaching children not to be ashamed of sex or of their own bodies. Sex as the celebration of life and love, as celebration of the body, of the glory of the Creator Spirit in us.

WARNINGS

To remember that the system—the government and the police and all the people who are crazy about money, who love money more than they love life—are going to tell the people that this idea can't work.

To remember that the old system is working away night and day to keep the people believing that force is necessary, that police and law and jails and money are necessary: that the old system has never imagined that it could be any other way. To remember that love can hardly express itself in a society where sex and love are repressed, and where money forces us to compete with each other all the time and sets us against each other.

To realize that we don't need to be divided up into nations. We are each born on this planet among the stars. We can work together and not against each other. To recognize war as the child of nationalism, of property, and of money, of systems that breed hatred.

That only the people have the strength that is needed: that only the people can free the people.

NOTE ON HISTORIC PRECEDENCE

What happened in the Ukraine in Russia between 1917-1921, and what happened in Spain in 1936-37: The farmers, the people who are close to the earth and the natural way of doing things, found it very easy very quickly to get together and form collectives, to get rid of any form of local government, to hold the land collectively, work it collectively, to supply their own needs, and to increase production so that they could take larger amounts of food than ever before to the cities. Some of them even went so far as to abolish money in their villages, and reports about them indicate that they experienced the return into their midst of long exiled joy.

122

The maximum happiness of one depends on the maximum happiness of all. Jose Oiticica.

And life, or what we call life, is becoming less and less separable from thought. Artaud.

In the revolution these two realities dissolve in each other:

The disalienation of the people from each other: the creation at last of a holy body of thought and action (life) which cannot be separate from the people, which is the people.

The misery of body and of mind resolve in our disalienation from each other.

This unification cannot be accomplished in an oppressed condition where movement and thought are suppressed.

Press up. Uprising.

The question, 1972, is how?

The only answer, 1972, is in starting now. How? Mobilization for total revolution.

To see around corners, thru things. Vision that penetrates opacity. But how can we be sure of this? The ear. Listen. Hearing the sounds that gird the earth. *Om. Sh'ma.* Hear.

Class division as a primary split. Destruction of the unity. Fractured cosmos located in class system.

Closed, private: the quality of the bourgeois person: closets, locks, keys that shut things in and are not to open: private property: removed from the mass. held apart: God dwells in the people. Not in things.

First: to become conscious of our condition, of being under arrest, of our class. Second: eclipse of class. Third: How? Uprising.

To establish our identity as people we have to destroy the hatefilled world of nationalism in which we are divided from each other. Unification. We go from land to land, not from "country to country," to re-create our identity as a people: for holiness is in the midst of people and not ever in the midst of a nation.

The life of the theatre.

We expect life to come: life will come when we summon it. Love. When we no longer reject it. End of loneliness. The endless beginning. The ocean. At last. Of life.

The longing of our hearts, the request of our lips, the merit of our hands.

Therefore each one may say, "The world was created for my sake"; and the people may say, "The world was created for all."

123

Night. Dreams. Mutiny. Night. Night. Working. Always. Mutiny. Slave uprising. Night. Mutiny. Jail. I am talking about life and death. Talking. Writing. Night. Circles. Circular dreams. Prison. In prison we become the prisoners even of our dreams. I dream of escape but it is always a dream. Night. Working. Working. Escape. Escape. Jail. Night. Jail. Night. Trap. Night. Mutiny. Uprising.

Uprising. How?

Infuse. Study. Organize. Mobilize. To love. Act.

To break out of the prison, the theatre, into the world.

Detention Cells. D.O.P.S. (Departamento de Ordem Politica e Social). Belo Horizonte, Brazil. 1 August 1971.